KT-477-293

INSIGHT ⊙ GUIDES

EXPLORE

CROATIA

15 355 412 7

⦿ Walking Eye App

Your guide now includes a free eBook to your chosen destination, for the same great price as before. Simply download the Walking Eye App from the App Store or Google Play to access your free eBook.

HOW THE WALKING EYE APP WORKS

Through the Walking Eye App, you can purchase a range of eBooks and destination content. However, when you buy this book, you can download the corresponding eBook for free. Just see below in the grey panel where to find your free content and then scan the QR code at the bottom of this page.

Destinations: Download essential destination content featuring recommended sights and attractions, restaurants, hotels and an A–Z of practical information, all available for purchase.

Ships: Interested in ship reviews? Find independent reviews of river and ocean ships in this section, all available for purchase.

eBooks: You can download your free accompanying digital version of this guide here. You will also find a whole range of other eBooks, all available for purchase.

Free access to travel-related blog articles about different destinations, updated on a daily basis.

HOW THE EBOOKS WORK

The eBooks are provided in EPUB file format. Please note that you will need an eBook reader installed on your device to open the file. Many devices come with this as standard, but you may still need to install one manually from Google Play.

The eBook content is identical to the content in the printed guide.

HOW TO DOWNLOAD THE WALKING EYE APP

1. Download the Walking Eye App from the App Store or Google Play.
2. Open the app and select the scanning function from the main menu.
3. Scan the QR code on this page – you will then be asked a security question to verify ownership of the book.
4. Once this has been verified, you will see your eBook in the purchased ebook section, where you will be able to download it.

Other destination apps and eBooks are available for purchase separately or are free with the purchase of the Insight Guide book.

CONTENTS

ARCHITECTURE

Fortified Dubrovnik (route 12) is architecturally unique. Rovinj (route 5), Trogir (route 8), Hvar (route 11) and Korčula (route 15) are Renaissance jewels, while Zagreb (routes 1 and 2) mixes the medieval and the 19th century.

RECOMMENDED ROUTES FOR...

OUTDOOR TYPES

Work up a sweat climbing Biokovo Mountain (route 8), or for a gentler workout, swim and cycle on Mljet (route 13) or Hvar (route 11). Rovinj (route 5) offers several activities including rock-climbing, scuba-diving and swimming.

BEACHES

The best sandy beaches are those of Pelješac (route 14), Lopud (route 12), Lumbarda on Korčula (route 15) and the Pakleni islands (route 11). Mljet (route 13) and Vis (route 10) have quieter options.

NATIONAL PARKS

For unspoilt natural beauty, try Krka (route 9) with its island monastery and waterfalls, the striking Plitvice Lakes (route 4) and verdant Mljet (route 13) with two saltwater lakes and lush forests.

FOODIES

A stay in Croatia would not be complete without sampling wine from the Pelješac peninsula (route 14), truffles from Istria (route 6) and seafood from Mali Ston (route 14). Zagreb (routes 1 and 2) has excellent restaurants.

ROMAN RUINS

Diocletian's Palace in Split (route 7) retains most of the grandeur of the original imperial palace. It is easy to imagine gladiatorial combat in the Roman amphitheatre of Pula (route 5).

CHILDREN

Kids love the beach, but they will also be awed by the waterfalls of Plitvice Lakes (route 4) and Krka National Park (route 9). The castles of Zagorje (route 3) are straight out of a fairy tale.

NIGHT OWLS

The most diverse nightlife is in Zagreb (routes 1 and 2), with everything from jazz clubs to discos. Hvar Town (route 11) has the trendiest cocktail scene, and Split (route 7) has a Mediterranean vibe.

INTRODUCTION

An introduction to Croatia's geography, customs and culture, plus illuminating background information on cuisine, history and what to do when you're there.

Croatia's coastline is dotted with myriad islands

EXPLORE CROATIA

Croatia is one of Europe's most exciting destinations, with a seemingly endless coastline, hundreds of islands and the kind of laid-back attitude that makes for a great holiday. History, culture, beaches: Croatia has it all.

Perhaps one of Croatia's best attributes is that you get two countries for the price of one. The long coastal region is heavily influenced by Italy, from the cuisine and Roman ruins to the insouciant attitude. Zagreb and northern Croatia, on the other hand, have much closer cultural, linguistic and economic ties with Germany and Austria which are demonstrated, in particular, by the Baroque cities that flourished in the 17th and 18th centuries under Austro-Hungarian rule. This duality is a direct result of Croatia's tortuous history.

CROATIAN IDENTITY

The great epoch of Croatian kings was more than 1,000 years ago. For many centuries, a country called 'Croatia' simply didn't exist. The Adriatic coast was part of the Roman Empire and then the Byzantine Empire before bouncing over to Hungarian kings and then the Venetians, the French (under Napoleon Bonaparte) and Italy in the 20th century. Austrians and Hungarians exerted nearly continuous control over the interior until the end of World War I when the first Kingdom of Serbs, Croats and

Slovenes emerged, later supplanted by Yugoslavia at the end of World War II (see page 24). During all of this, a sense of national identity was somehow kept alive throughout Croatia's diverse regions. The Serbian nationalism of Slobodan Milošević provided the spark that fired up Croatia's long-suppressed dream of independence. Nevertheless, the resulting conflagration took most Croatians by surprise. The terrible war years were followed by economic stagnation. But in spite of a long and difficult journey, independent Croatia has regained its footing and became a member of the European Union in 2013.

GEOGRAPHY AND LAYOUT

Covering 56,538 sq km (21,830 sq miles), Croatia can be divided into three regions: the lowland basin between the Sava and Drava rivers, which includes Zagreb and then rises to the northern hills of the Zagorje; the Dinaric mountains that rise so dramatically from the coast; and the long littoral that stretches along the Adriatic. In terms of popularity among visitors, the coast is a clear winner. From Istria to Dubrovnik,

Split, one of the Adriatic's liveliest and most alluring cities

it runs 1,778km (1,105 miles), while 1,185 offshore islands and islets provide innumerable opportunities for sport and relaxation.

Zagreb and northern Croatia

Too few people spend time in this part of the country. Zagreb has everything you could hope for in a Central European capital: museums, fine restaurants, exciting nightlife and a typical mixture of Baroque and Secessionist architecture. During the Yugoslav years, when Zagreb was playing second fiddle to Belgrade, this repository of Croatian culture languished. Now it is rushing to flash its newfound prosperity. Women in the latest fashions crowd into trendy boutiques or linger over cocktails in sleek cafés, while men in designer sunglasses emerge from Italian sports cars. Yet there is also a more bohemian side, evident in the funky cafés and clubs of Zagreb's medieval Upper Town.

The city makes a great base from which to venture into the cool hills of the Zagorje region to the north. Here the farmers are only a generation removed from cart-and-horse transport. It was from this region that the Croatian nobility once reigned; a visit to their turreted castles is a trip to the heart of the Croatian national identity.

Istria

There are still old-timers in Istria who have lived in four countries without ever leaving their homeland. They were Austrians until 1918, Italians until 1945, Yugoslavs until 1991 and finally Croatians. The turmoil has left Istrians with a philosophical view of history, an agility with languages and a welcoming attitude towards visitors. The last has helped to make the region a choice European destination for second residences and retirement homes. Of course, a mild climate, reasonable cost of living, delicious food and a long coastline also help Istria's popularity.

Split and the Dalmatian coast

The inhabitants of Croatia's second city are full of pride. They are proud of their football team, Hajduk Split; proud of producing fine tennis players such as Goran Ivanišević and Mario Ančić; and proud of the city's easy blend of ancient and modern. The Unesco-protected

A narrow, cobbled street in Rovinj

Plitvice National Park

Diocletian's Palace draws visitors, but the ebullient Split lifestyle keeps them happy. Stroll along the seafront promenade, while away time in a local café, or join the frenetic nightlife scene to understand why Split residents are so passionate about their city.

Split's location makes it easy to sample other appealing destinations on the Dalmatian coast, whether your interests are cultural or veer towards outdoorsy activities. The ancient Roman ruins of Salona are a haunting evocation of a vanished world, and the majestic waterfalls of Krka National Park are an enchanting place to spend the day. The World Heritage Site of Trogir is a jewel of a medieval town, while Makarska is at the foot of the towering Biokovo Mountain.

Mali Ston is famous for its oysters

Islands

Croatia is the proud possessor of some of the world's most beautiful islands. Years of 'neglect' have made Vis the best get-away-from-it-all island, while Mljet is truly an island paradise with sandy beaches, forested hills and inland lakes. Korčula is steeped in the tradition of cultivating olive trees and vineyards and has a picturesque Old Town to explore. Hvar has lavender fields, an offshore constellation of islands and hyper-trendy nightlife in Hvar Town.

Dubrovnik

The 'pearl of the Adriatic' according to Lord Byron, Dubrovnik is Croatia's crown jewel. The walled city appears to be sculpted rather than built, with monuments, fountains and landmarks of astonishing beauty. A wealth of museums and monasteries traces its fascinating history and unique culture, and it is easy to visit the region it once ruled, such as the Pelješac peninsula with the 'great wall' of Ston or the peaceful Elaphiti islands.

CLIMATE

As well as two cultures, Croatia has two distinct climates. Along the coast the climate is Mediterranean, with hot and dry summers, although the *bura* wind blowing from the mountains refreshes summer afternoons. Winters are rainy, but the Dinaric mountain range protects the coast from harsh weather. The coast

Diocletian's Palace, Split

Basilica of St Euphrasius mosaic, Poreč

from Dubrovnik to Split tends to be one or two degrees warmer than the northern Dalmatian coast up to Istria. Hvar island is the sunniest spot in Croatia.

Inland Croatia has a continental climate. Zagreb and the interior forests are occasionally blanketed with snow, and freezing temperatures are not uncommon from December to the end of February.

WHEN TO GO

Croatia can be appreciated in any season, but most people come in July and August. The weather is reliably sunny; attractions are open for longer hours and there are more boats to whisk you from island to island. May, June and September are less crowded, though, and you can still see

DON'T LEAVE CROATIA WITHOUT...

Exploring Plitvice Lakes National Park. The 16 lakes and countless waterfalls of this Unesco site are in a stunning shade of turquoise, and are easily explored via wooden walkways and ferries. Head to the upper lakes for a wilder experience. See page 40.

Walking Dubrovnik's walls. Take a stroll around these magnificent medieval fortifications for an intimate look at the inner life of the city, as well as beautiful panoramic views. See page 80.

Mellowing out in Mljet. This tranquil green island north of Dubrovnik has two saltwater lakes, lush forests and plenty of footpaths and trails for cycling and hiking. Hire a scooter to reach the best beaches. See page 88.

Living like a Roman emperor. Diocletian's Palace in Split is one of Croatia's most unusual sights, a crumbling third-century palace whose ruins have long housed apartments, shops and restaurants. See page 57.

Tasting the high life in Hvar. The sophisticated nightlife in this sunny Dalmatian island has made it one of the most popular spots along the Adriatic coast for late-night cocktails and clubbing. See page 74.

Savouring Zagreb's café society. They take coffee seriously in Croatia's capital, where the café functions both as a gossip hub and a place to see and be seen. See page 31.

Eating the 'world's best oysters'. Mali Ston's oysters were officially given this title back in 1936 by the General Trades International Exhibition in London. Certainly this part of the Pelješac peninsula is one of the loveliest spots for seafood and excellent white wines. See page 93.

Perching in Istria's hill towns. Inland Istria is an enchanting landscape of hills, valleys, vineyards and woods. Its hilltop towns are exquisite, including Motovun, home to a summer film festival, and Grožnjan, with its artists' colony. See page 52.

Admiring Byzantine art. While the seaside Istrian resort of Poreč is a favourite with holidaymakers, its basilica is home to a remarkable collection of Byzantine art and gold-studded mosaics. See page 46.

Dolac Market in Zagreb, with its distinctive red umbrellas

and do a lot. By October, many islanders turn from receiving guests to harvesting their olives or grapes, so it is a great time to experience an age-old way of life.

Winter is too cold for swimming in the sea, but Dubrovnik is just as enchanting, and you can share it with residents rather than other tourists. Meanwhile, Zagreb's cultural season is in full swing, and you can ski just outside town. Spring is the best time to visit Plitvice Lakes and Krka National Park, as the cascades are swollen with the melting winter snows.

PEOPLE

Croatia's population has declined from five million, when it was part of the former Yugoslavia, to 4.2 million today. During the 1990s war, much of the Serbian population left or was chased out. The return of Serbian refugees has been slow, partly because of the web of legal

Fishermen in Rovinj harbour

problems involved in reclaiming their former property. Also, in some parts of the country, bitter feelings and troubled local economies remain from the war years, which means the environment is less than welcoming for returning Serbs.

Another challenge to population stability is the increasing desire of young people to look for opportunities abroad. Croatia has a long history of exporting its people, from political refugees fleeing Tito to providing labour for the growing post-war economies of Italy and Germany. Croatia's historical ties abroad make it easy for multilingual young people to find higher-paid jobs elsewhere, and many of them choose to do so.

Religion
Croatians are overwhelmingly – nearly 88 percent – Roman Catholic. In fact, the defining characteristic of Croats is adherence to the Roman Catholic faith, while Serbs belong to the Eastern Orthodox Church. During the Tito years, religious practices were discouraged – if not banned – in an attempt to dampen down the nationalistic feelings they so often inspired. Since independence, Croatians have celebrated religious holidays with fervour, and the Catholic Church holds a central place in community life.

Traditions and customs
Croatians are keen to display their rich cultural heritage. Communities have no trouble in persuading citizens to join in historical re-enactments, participate in

Selling rakija in Krka National Park

folk-dancing events and keep alive the traditions of the forefathers, which differ between regions and even between islands. Many festivities take place around Easter, and are connected with local saints' days and historical events. One of the most colourful local displays is the weekly Moreška sword dance in Korčula.

TOP TIPS FOR EXPLORING CROATIA

Bring swimming shoes. Pebbly beaches outnumber sandy ones in Croatia, and it's much easier to enjoy the waters if your feet are protected. All of the resorts sell neoprene-style shoes cheaply.

'Under the dome'. When in Croatia, you're bound to hear of food cooked under a cast-iron dome called a *peka*. Meat (*meso ispod peke*) and vegetables are cooked under this dome and buried in glowing embers. The results melt in the mouth. It's also a delicious way of baking bread.

Clothing optional. Naturist beaches are common in Croatia, and the tradition goes back nearly a century. Look out for signs saying FKK – an abbreviation taken from the German for Free Body Culture – if you wish to strip off or avoid the beach altogether.

City cards. Tourist passes in Zagreb and Dubrovnik are good value for money if you plan to spend more than a day there. They include free admission to many attractions and on transport, as well as discounts in restaurants and shops.

Time for lunch. Mealtimes are almost any time of the day, apart from a few expensive establishments that don't serve between 3pm and 7pm. Many Croatians work from 7am to 3pm and will eat lunch then.

Go to market. The daily food markets all around Croatia are a treat, and worth exploring before they pack up at lunchtime. Only a few will remain open all day.

Island hopping. It's hard to resist the temptation to explore some of Croatia's 1,000-plus islands, and along certain parts of the coast it's feasible to see quite a few in one holiday. Check the website of ferry company Jadrolinija for schedules, and bear in mind that frequency drops off dramatically beyond the main summer season.

Carnival time. While parts of the country can be a bit sleepy in late winter, everyone perks up for the pre-Lent carnival season. Dubrovnik, Split and Rijeka host some of the liveliest carnivals in Europe.

Sun and heat. Temperatures can reach 40°C (104°F) in the summer, so protect yourself from the sun. Many Croatian beaches, both on the mainland and in the islands, are backed by pine groves where you can find some respite from the heat.

Avoid the crowds. During the height of the tourist season, up to seven cruise ships a day can descend on Dubrovnik – swelling tourist numbers by as many as 7,000, with most trying to squeeze into the Old Town. The majority of cruise passengers will have returned to their ships by late afternoon, so that's the best time to relax in the Old Town after you've spent the day in the beaches in Babin Kuk or Lapad.

Seafood fresh from the Adriatic

FOOD AND DRINK

From fresh fish and locally produced olive oil to fine wines and garden–fresh vegetables, Croatian cuisine is simple but delicious and healthy. Moreover, you can eat and drink extraordinarily well on a reasonable budget.

Many people are surprised by the quality of Croatian cuisine. Along the Adriatic, the Italian influence is evident in the excellent pizza and pasta dishes that are everywhere; the menus also emphasise the bounty of the sea with a profusion of fish and seafood dishes. In the interior, the menus are much more Central European, with hearty stews, roasted meat dishes and cream pastries.

WHERE TO EAT

In addition to restaurants, there are family-run establishments called *gostionice* or *konobe*. A typical *konoba* (or *klet* in Zagorje) can be anything from a small enterprise serving local wine and salty delicacies such as *slane srdele* (salted sardines), *dalmatinski pršut* (Dalmatian ham) and *sir* (cheese) to a full-blown restaurant, though usually with a simple menu.

A *pivnica* is an informal pub that usually does not serve food, and a *kavana* is a café that serves only drinks, cakes and ice cream. You can also satisfy your sweet tooth in a *slastičarna*, which offers cake, strudel and ice cream to take away.

WHAT TO EAT

For breakfast, try a *burek*, a meat- or cheese-filled filo pastry. Except in touristy areas, it is impossible to find anything resembling an English breakfast.

Seafood
In Istria and Dalmatia, seafood tops the menu, and fish and shellfish are invariably prepared with abundant quantities of olive oil, parsley and garlic. Favourite starters include *salat od hobotnice* (octopus salad) and *dagnje* (mussels). In the Limska kanal region of Istria and Mali Ston in Dalmatia, you will also find *oštrige* (oysters). *Crni rižot*, a delicious black risotto cooked in cuttlefish ink, or the more delicate *škampi rižot* made with shrimps' tails, can be found on almost every menu.

Fish come in two categories: white fish such as *zubatac orada* (gilthead), *šampier* (John Dory), *trilja* (red mullet), *škarpina* (grouper) and *arbun* (sea bream); and cheaper 'blue' fish, notably *tunj* (tuna), *skuše* (mackerel) and *srdele* (sardines). Both types are often prepared on a *roštilj* (barbecue), and served with *mješenji salat* (mixed salad) or *blitva* (swiss chard

Pancakes for dessert

Enjoying a local red

smothered in olive oil and garlic). *Ligne* (squid), *škampi na buzara* (shrimps cooked in tomato sauce) and *brodet* (fish soup) are also favourites. Mljet is known for its excellent *jastog* (lobster).

Meat

Croatian meat is locally produced and often free range, with *janjetina* (lamb) the most popular type. In the hinterland, many roadside restaurants display whole lambs as well as pigs roasting on a spit. Zagorje is renowned for *puretina* (turkey), *patka* (duck) and *guska* (goose). Other notable meat dishes are Hungarian *gulaš*, and *pašticada*, a Dalmatian beef stew.

Vegetarians

While vegetarians can eat well, they do not have a lot to choose from. Nevertheless, simply prepared, locally grown vegetables topped with local olive oil are full of flavour. Salads are on most menus, and vegetable pizzas are readily available.

Dessert

The most popular Croatian desserts include *palačinke* (thin pancakes) topped with chocolate, walnuts, ice cream or other treats, and various *štrudle* (pies) filled with *jabuka* (apple), *trešnja* (cherry) or *sir* (cheese). *Štrukli*, made from curd cheese folded into dough, then boiled and served with toasted or fried breadcrumbs, is a speciality of Zagorje. Try salty *štrukli* as a starter and sugary *štrukli* for dessert. *Sladoled* (ice cream) is almost as popular on the eastern Adriatic as in Italy. The Turks brought baklava to the Balkans, as well as *burek* and *čevapčići* (meat rissoles).

WHAT TO DRINK

Croatians are apt to start the day with a strong cup of espresso or cappuccino. In hot weather, it is common to linger over an iced Nescafé – cold coffee with milk and ice cream.

Meals often start with a small glass of *rakija*, made from distilled alcohol flavoured with fruits or herbs. The best known are *travarica*, which takes its taste from aromatic grasses, and amber-coloured *pelinkovac*, which is bitter. The speciality on Vis is carob-based *rogačica*, while in inland Istria you will come across *biska*, made from mistletoe. In Lika (the mountainous central region that includes the Plitvice Lakes), try plum-based *šljivovica*.

The best Istrian wines are the white Malvazija and the red Teran. Dalmatian wines tend to be heavier and stronger. The best known are the full-bodied reds: Dingač from Pelješac peninsula, and Plavac from Hvar and Vis. The best whites are Pošip Čara from Hvar and Grk from Korčula. Prošek, a sweet wine made from sun-dried grapes, is a customary digestif.

Beer-drinkers can try the two major brands: Ožujsko from Zagreb and Karlovačko from Karlovac, south of the capital. Tap water is drinkable.

Lavender is a popular souvenir

SHOPPING

There are designer and international brands available, but uniquely Croatian items offer better value for money. Souvenirs are of most interest to the majority of visitors, from textiles to jewellery, and ceramics to perfumes.

The Croatian manufacturing industry all but collapsed after the 1990s war: cosmetics, clothes and household goods are now largely imported, hence the extremely high prices and a tottering national economy. Many Croatians take 'shopping buses' to Trieste in Italy and Graz in Austria. Nevertheless, you will find excellent food and drink, as well as various traditional handmade products that make unusual gifts to take home.

WINE AND SPIRITS

Croatia has been cultivating grapes since the Roman era, and the quality of wine can be excellent (see page 17).

You will find a wide range of Croatian wines and *rakija* in Vinoteka Bornstein (Kaptol 19; www.bornstein.hr) in Zagreb, all beautifully displayed in a large vaulted brick cellar. In Istria, try Enoteka Vinoteka Sempervivum (www.sempervivum.hr) in Veleniki near Poreč, where you can try the wine in the original 19th-century tavern. In Split, call in at Enoteca Terra (Braće Kaliterne 6) close to Bačvica Bay, which is both a shop and a wine bar where you can taste before you buy. In Dubrovnik, Dubrovačka Kuća (Sv. Dominika 2) sells wine, *rakija* and olive oil.

Markets

Wherever you go, allow some time to visit the local open-air market, where you will find a colourful array of stalls laden with seasonal fruit and vegetables that are bursting with taste. Honey is not the easiest thing to pack in your suitcase, but you may well be tempted to buy some from beekeepers who display their produce on small wooden stands. Slightly more manageable while travelling are non-perishable goods: look out for dried figs, walnuts, strings of garlic and bunches of dried hot red peppers. Herbal teas are popular for therapeutic purposes; there seems to be one for every ailment. Markets invariably feature an elderly lady bartering bags of sun-dried *šipak* (rosehip), *kamomil* (camomile), *menta* (mint) and *kadulja* (sage), all of which are far more flavoursome than the prepacked varieties. Food markets tend to be open only in the mornings, even in more touristy areas.

Zigante Tartufi truffle sauce

Gingerbread hearts for sale in Kumrovec

FOOD

Other foodstuffs include *pršut* (ham) and *paški sir* (sheep's cheese from the island of Pag). Check customs restrictions before you bring them home, though. Along the coast you can buy *maslinovo ulje* (olive oil), although it can be more expensive here than in Italy. For the best deal, go direct to a producer, who will let you try some before you decide to buy. Truffles are good value, however, and connoisseurs can choose from both the black and the white varieties of this earthy delicacy that are an Istrian speciality. Indeed, the world's biggest truffle, weighing 1.31kg (3lb), was found by Giancarlo Zigante near Buje in Istria in 1999. Look out for Zigante Tartufi shops in a number of Istria towns (see www. zigantetartufi.com), and the Zigante restaurant in Livade (see page 55).

SOUVENIRS

Handicrafts

Craftsmanship is highly valued in Croatia, and many souvenirs are still made by hand.

In Istria you might like to buy a *bukaleta*, a traditional terracotta jug for serving wine, which can be found in souvenir shops in Poreč and Rovinj. Here you will also find ceramic models of *kažuni*, the round stone huts seen in this region.

In the south you can buy replicas of traditional Dalmatian stone houses. The best place to shop for handmade gifts in Split is in the Podrum, the underground gallery leading from the seafront to the Peristyle. Dubrovnik was renowned for its goldsmiths and silversmiths, and today filigree jewellery is a speciality. A number of jewellers around Od Puča sell modern as well as old and antique pieces.

If visiting Zagorje and the Zagreb area, you can buy a *licitarsko srce*, a gingerbread heart decorated with icing and a ribbon. Years ago, men would give these to the girl they loved on Valentine's Day. You will find shops selling these gifts in Zagreb, close to Trg bana Josipa Jelačića, and also in Kumrovec, Zagorje.

Natural products

You can pick up sponges at reasonable prices in souvenir shops in Šibenik. They come from the nearby island of Krapanj, where they have been the main source of income for generations.

Visitors to the island of Hvar will be struck by the lavender-scented air. In the summer you can buy dried lavender and lavender perfume from all main tourist centres.

Alternatively, take home the summer fragrances of the Dalmatian islands by shopping at Aromatica (www.aromatica. hr), which produces herbal soaps, natural skin creams, massage oils and teas, and has shops in Zagreb (Vlaška 7) and Rovinj (Garibaldi 20).

Folk performance in Split's Diocletian's Palace

ENTERTAINMENT

Culturally, there is plenty going on in Croatia. Music-lovers are well catered for – the summer music festival season is expanding every year, and there are classical concerts in all major cities. Jazz is growing in popularity, and nightclubs spin all the latest sounds.

THE ARTS

Concerts, opera and plays offer excellent value for money, as tickets are relatively cheap and the quality is high. Croatians became used to government subsidies for the arts under the Yugoslav regime, and still expect to have their tastes satisfied at a relatively low cost. They take pride in supporting Croatian composers and musicians, even though few have attained international renown.

Zagreb, Split and Dubrovnik are the major cultural centres where you can hear first-rate musicians and singers perform. Zagreb has its own opera, theatre and ballet company (check www.hnk.hr for schedules), and the major concert hall is the Vatroslav Lisinski (www.lisinski.hr). Dubrovnik even has its own symphony orchestra (www.dso.hr), which is a remarkable show of support for the arts considering the size of the town. The concert, ballet and opera season runs from October until May, which is another good reason to come to Croatia off-season.

CINEMA

Croatia has a growing cinema scene, although foreign blockbusters tend to crowd out Croatian films in local cinemas. Foreign films are always shown in the original language with subtitles. In the summer, many resorts offer open-air cinema – some in picturesque ancient sites – with projections commencing after sunset.

CROATIAN MUSIC

One of the most popular forms of folk music is *klapa*, when a group of men or women sing a cappella in harmony. The music is haunting and expressive. You do not need to understand the words in order to be affected by the themes of love (often for the homeland) and loss. *Klapa* is particularly popular in Dalmatia and it is not confined to professional performances; the songs are widely known, and sung whenever a group of people is in the mood.

Croatian pop stars enjoy a huge following at home and throughout the former Yugoslavia. Tereza Kesovija, Oliver Dragojević, Severina and Gibonni are some of the artists whose music is frequently on the radio. It is worth checking out their concerts.

Pag Island, Croatia's answer to Ibiza

FESTIVALS

July and August are replete with music festivals. The most prestigious is the Dubrovnik Summer Festival (www.dubrovnik-festival.hr), which attracts artists – particularly classical musicians and actors – of the highest calibre. Medieval palaces, fortresses and courtyards provide delightful backdrops to the outdoor performances. It is also a good time to catch an off-season concert by the Dubrovnik Symphony Orchestra, and there are also plenty of visiting orchestras and soloists from around Europe. The programme includes top-notch folk performances, too. One perennial favourite is the Lado Ensemble of Zagreb, composed of highly accomplished singers and dancers versed in the Croatian folk tradition.

Another great summer event is the Split Summer Festival (www.splitskoljeto.hr), which presents a variety of concerts, plays and exhibitions around town. Open-air opera on the Peristyle is the main attraction, with a Verdi opera always topping the bill.

Istria also has its culture-fests. During June there are Music Evenings in Grožnjan, with Grožnjan Music Summer School concerts through to August. In nearby Motovun, a film festival is held in late July (www.motovunfilmfestival.com). The Pula Summer Festival is more pop-oriented, with an emphasis on Croatian entertainers. The festival venue is Pula's Roman amphitheatre, which is also frequently the site of shows throughout the year (www.histriafestival.com).

Poreč hosts jazz concerts in the courtyard of the Baroque Sinčić Palace in June and July, and the Basilica of St Euphrasius holds classical recitals from June to September.

Korčula is known for its festivals and its desire to keep traditions alive. The most important celebration is the Moreška, or Sword Dance Festival, held on St Theodor's Day (29 July), when lavishly dressed 'medieval knights' perform a stylised dance and play. A shortened version of the dance takes place on an outdoor stage at the Old Town gate every Thursday in summer (enquire at the tourist office for details).

Electronic music festivals have been popping up all along the Adriatic over the past decade. Earlier ones such as the Garden Festival near Zadar have been replaced by many others, including Ultra Europe in Split, and Soundwave and SunćeBeat in Tisno.

NIGHTCLUBS

The wildest and most varied nightlife is found in Zagreb, which has everything from jazz clubs to mega-discos. In summer the scene travels to the coast and islands. The summer nightlife capital is trendy Hvar Town with its chic clubs, but there are also vast open-air discos in Split and on Pag island. Pula has the most popular nightlife in Istria, often based on Verudela peninsula. For nightlife and entertainment listings, see page 120.

Cycling on Hvar island

OUTDOOR ACTIVITIES

Scuba–diving, sailing, windsurfing and swimming in the coastal waters attract most visitors, but Croatia's interior also provides an armful of opportunities to get physical, with hiking, rock–climbing and cycling.

You could simply relax on a beach and take occasional dips in the sea, but if you have a more active holiday in mind, Croatia offers a wealth of choice. Croatians love the outdoors and take full advantage of their mountains and sea, so participating in an activity is also a good way to meet locals. Tourist offices will have detailed information on sporting associations, equipment rental and routes.

CLIMBING

The karstic stone of Croatia's coastline is great for climbers. The caves and canyons of Paklenica National Park, near Zadar, make up one of the most important climbing sites in the country, popular with climbers at all levels. Contact the Visitors' Centre (tel: 023-369 155; www.paklenica.hr). Other climbing sites include Biokovo Nature Park and Marjan hill, Split.

CYCLING

In summer you can hire mountain bikes in all the main tourist centres. Central Istria has a number of well-maintained cycle paths; the Istria Tourist Board pro-

duces a comprehensive map of cycling routes, including distances, time, altitude and difficulty (www.istria-bike.com). The disused Trieste-Poreč railway track (the Parenzana) hosts numerous cycling events for amateurs, as well as a stage of the Tour of Croatia for professional racers (www.parenzana.com).

Hvar has allocated a number of minor roads and tracks to mountain biking; the tourist office has details. Mljet's excellent cycle paths run through the national park's dense forests and around the lakes.

DIVING

More thrills await underwater. Scuba-diving is superb along the Croatian coast, and there are dive centres on nearly every island and in most coastal towns. The primary dive highlights are caves and shipwrecks. The caves are a feature of Croatia's karstic rock, and the shipwrecks are a result of the powerful navies that once fought for dominance of the Adriatic. The most famous shipwreck is the *Baron Gautsch* near Rovinj (see page 48), but there are plenty of others. Vis island is known for its waters that teem

Croatia is a diver's delight

Sailing in Vis

with fish, as the island was off-limits for many years (see page 70). For more details see the national tourist board's diving pages (www.croatia.hr).

HIKING

The Dinaric mountains running parallel to the coast are a popular destination for hikers. There are a number of mountain huts, especially in the Velebit range north of Zadar, that provide simple but adequate lodging; it is wise to reserve in advance on summer weekends. Hiking paths are marked with a white dot within a red circle, but in more remote areas the markings have worn away or been removed by shepherds. The best hiking spot in southern Dalmatia is Biokovo Mountain. If you start early, you can make it to the top of the 1,762m (5,778ft) Sveti Jure peak in one day. Biokovo Active Holidays (tel: 021-679 655; www.biokovo.net) organises guided hikes in central Dalmatia.

Hvar island is a good choice for easier walks, and it's perfect for the warm summer season or for casual hikers Hvar Adventure (tel: 021-717 813; www.hvar-adventure.com) organises hiking tours all around the island, as well as kayaking, climbing and sailing programmes.

SAILING

Croatia truly is a sailor's paradise; indeed, the best way to appreciate its islands is by boat, as you can explore those that are inaccessible by ferry. Most of the islands mentioned in this book have agencies that rent small motorboats for the day, but you may want to see more. Those without sailing experience can opt for a skippered boat, but those with nautical experience can go 'bareboat'. (You will need to produce a valid recreational boat licence as well as a radio certificate.) Contact the Adriatic Club International (ACI), whose head office is in Opatija (tel: 052-271 288; www.aci-club.hr).

SWIMMING

For those who enjoy swimming in the sea, the Adriatic is a dream. From Istria to Dubrovnik, there is nothing but clean water with average temperatures of 23–26°C (73–79°F) in summer. The water can stay warm enough for swimming until October. There are so many sheltered coves that currents are rarely a problem, and the only dangerous sea creatures are urchins. Few beaches are sandy, however, and some are quite rocky.

WINDSURFING

The most popular windsurfing site in Croatia, for those visitors who are really serious about their sport, is at Bol, on Brač island, where the winds are reliably good from May to October. Viganj, in the southwest of the Pelješac peninsula (see page 92), and the Premantura peninsula outside Pula are also good windsurfing areas. For more information, check www.windsurfing.hr and www.orca-sport.com.

The Temple of Augustus in Pula

HISTORY: KEY DATES

Croatia's history is a turbulent one. Over the years, invading armies gobbled up territory only to be pushed out by other armies. All were vying for the fertile interior as well as the long coastline that was so essential for commercial and military control of the Adriatic.

EARLY PERIOD

1000BC	Illyrians arrive on Balkan peninsula.
4th century BC	First Greek colonies are founded on Adriatic islands, notably on Vis.
1st century BC	Romans arrive in Dalmatia and Istria. Interior remains Illyrian.
AD395	Roman territory is divided into Western and Eastern empires.
555	Istrian and Dalmatian coast become part of Byzantine Empire.
7th century	Slavs arrive on Balkan peninsula.
925	King Tomislav unites Dalmatia and Pannonia.
1054	Christian Church is divided between Rome and Constantinople.

RISE OF EMPIRES

1091	Croatia signs Pacta Conventa, recognising Hungarian royalty in return for self-government under a viceroy.
1240	Tatar invasion of Central Europe; destruction throughout Croatia.
1358	Birth of Republic of Ragusa (Dubrovnik).
1420	Venice takes Istrian and Dalmatian coasts.
16th century	Turks take Slavonia, Dalmatian hinterland and unprotected coastal towns. Austria develops Krajina military border.
1699	Croatia is liberated from Turkish rule. The Habsburgs take Pannonia; Venice takes Dalmatia. Only Dubrovnik is independent.

AUSTRO-HUNGARIAN RULE

1797	Venetian Republic ends. Dalmatia and Istria come under Austro-Hungarian control.
1805	Napoleon unites Dalmatia, Istria and much of Slovenia under the Illyrian Provinces.
1808	Republic of Dubrovnik is abolished.

Croatia joined the EU in 2013

1815	Fall of Napoleon. Dalmatia comes under Habsburg rule.
1881	Krajina is incorporated into Croatia.
1914	Shooting of Archduke Franz Ferdinand sparks World War I.

YUGOSLAVIA

1918	Croatia becomes part of Kingdom of Serbs, Croats and Slovenes under King Aleksandar, later assassinated by extremists in 1934.
1941	Germany declares war on Yugoslavia. Ustaše seizes power in Croatia. Tito forms Partisan movement.
1945	Tito founds Federal Democratic People's Republic of Yugoslavia with Croatia as one of the six republics.
1971	'Croatian Spring' fuels nationalist fervour. Agitators imprisoned.
1980	Tito dies. Yugoslavia is left with a system of rotating presidency.
1980s	Economic crisis sets in. Slovenia and Croatia object to funding poorer republics. Serbian nationalism grows.
1990	Franjo Tuđman is elected president with a nationalist manifesto.

WAR AND PEACE

1991	Croatia proclaims independence; Serb population proclaims Republic of Serbian Krajina, blockading a third of Croatia. War breaks out. Croats in Vukovar are among the worst casualties.
1992	EU and UN recognise Croatia. UN peacekeepers deployed to oversee ceasefire and protect Serb minority.
1995	Croats take back Serb-held areas of Slavonia and Krajina – thousands of Serbs are expelled.
1999	President Tuđman dies.

TOWARDS THE EU

2005	Former general Ante Gotovina is tried in The Hague for war crimes against the Krajina Serbs. He is found guilty in 2011, but the verdict is overturned in 2012.
2013	After settling dispute with Italy and Slovenia over Adriatic fishing rights, Croatia becomes the 28th member of the European Union.
2015	Kolinda Grabar-Kitarović becomes the first female President of Croatia, as well as the youngest at 46.

BEST ROUTES

Grapes for sale at the Dolac market

ZAGREB: UPPER TOWN

Stroll through Zagreb's Upper Town (Gornji grad), the oldest part of Croatia's capital city, with a look at the cathedral, the local market, historic monuments and the city's most appealing cafés.

DISTANCE: 2km (1 mile)
TIME: A half day; a full day with museum visits
START: Trg Bana Josipa Jelačića
END: Lotrščak Tower
POINTS TO NOTE: Do this tour in the morning to get the full flavour of Dolac and to arrive at Lotrščak Tower at noon in time for the firing of the cannon. It can then be combined with route 2 (the Lower Town) in the afternoon.

The history of Zagreb's Upper Town (Gornji grad) is a tale of two hilltop cities: Gradec and Kaptol. Kaptol was under the jurisdiction of the Church, while Gradec was controlled by the reigning monarch from the 13th to 17th centuries. Even now, Kaptol has a more sober look than leafy Gradec. The encroachment of the Turks in the 16th century forced the two communities to merge, but the new city was beset by fire and plague which sent the economy into a tailspin. In the 19th century, rail links put Zagreb at the crossroads of the Austro-Hungarian Empire; it grew prosperous, developing a flourishing cultural and intellectual life.

Zagreb took a back seat to Belgrade during the Yugoslav years, but has now re-established itself as one of Eastern Europe's most exciting cities, with world-class shopping, superb dining and a vibrant artistic scene.

KAPTOL

Start the morning with coffee at **Aïda Café Vienna** (see ①) on **Trg Bana Josipa Jelačića ①**.

Cathedral
Leave the square by the passage in the northeast corner in the direction of the church spires. Walk uphill about 50m/yds on Bakačeva until you reach, on the right, the **Cathedral of the Assumption of the Virgin Mary ②** (Katedrala Marijina Uznesenja; 7am–7.30pm; free) in the heart of Kaptol. The original building dates from the 12th century, but the neo-Gothic façade and twin bell towers were added by Viennese architect Hermann Bollé in the 19th century. Step inside

Inside the cathedral   Façades on Tkalčićeva

to see a medieval inscription of the Ten Commandments on the north wall. It is written in Glagolitic script, which dates from the ninth century (see page 54). Also on the north wall is the tomb of Cardinal Aloysius Stepinac, carved by Ivan Meštrović. Stepinac was the archbishop of Zagreb during World War II. He was beatified despite controversy surrounding his role under the Nazi puppet regime.

Walk north up Kaptol to Opatovina on the left and follow the street downhill past the cosy cafés. The street traces the line of the former walls that once surrounded Kaptol.

Belly of Zagreb

At the end of Opatovina is **Dolac** ❸

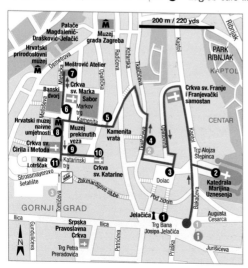

(Mon–Fri 7am–4pm, Sat–Sun 7am–2pm), the market known as the 'Belly of Zagreb', which opened in 1926. Colourful fruit and vegetable stalls occupy the open-air upper level, while below, an indoor market deals in dairy products, salamis, home-cured hams and a sumptuous array of breads and cakes. After a snack, leave Dolac by Tkalčićeva, one street west of Opatovina.

Café culture

Tkalčićeva ❹ was once a waterway that formed the boundary between Gradec and Kaptol. A stream flowed here, powering several mills, until 1898, when a street was built over it. Tkalčićeva is the pulse of Zagreb café life, a busy pedestrian zone lined with restaurants, bars and cafés with outdoor seating. Stop here for a *palačinke* (pancake) at **Kava Tava** (see ❷).

GRADEC

Turn left on Mlinarske stube and go up the steep wooden steps to Radićeva. Turn left and a short way down, on the right side of the street, is the pretty **Stone Gate** ❺ (Kamenita vrata), once the gate to Gradec. The original 13th-century town walls had four gates, of which only the Stone

A glimpse of St Mark's Church roof

Gate remains. Within the arched gateway stands an enchanting shrine to the Virgin Mary, full of flowers and candles.

St Mark's Square

Leave the gate on the other side at Kamenita ulica. Follow it to **Markov trg ⑥**, crowned by **St Mark's Church** (Crkva sv. Marka), with its extraordinary coloured roof. In contrast to St Catherine's, this church was erected as a humble place of prayer for the craftsmen of Gradec in the 13th century. In the 19th century, the church was subject to extensive reconstruction work, part of which gave it the Hungarian-style roof. The emblem on the roof's right side is that of the city of Zagreb. The emblem to the left represents the coat of arms of Croatia, Dalmatia and Slavonia, which originally made up the medieval kingdom.

The nation's governmental and administrative buildings are around Markov trg, hence the low-key police presence. On the eastern side of the square, behind the church, stands the **Parliament building** (Sabor), and on the western side stands the **Ban's Palace** (Banski dvorj), the seat of the Croatian government.

Meštrović Atelier

Pass through the square to the north to find Mletačka. At no. 8 stands the beautiful **Meštrović Atelier ⑦** (www.mdc.hr/mestrovic; Tue–Fri 10am–6pm, Sat–Sun 10am–2pm; charge). Often unjustly neglected by the international art world, Ivan Meštrović (1883–1962) deserves a place in the pantheon of the greatest sculptors of the 20th century. More than 100 figurative works – in wood, bronze and marble – are arranged informally throughout the artist's former home, studio and garden.

Croatian Museum of Naïve Art

Return to Markov trg and take Ćirilometodska on the opposite (southern) side to reach the **Croatian Museum of Naïve Art ⑧** (Hrvatski muzej naivne umjetnosti; www.hmnu.org; Tue–Fri 10am–6pm, Sat 10am–2pm; Sun 10am–1pm; charge) at no. 3. Unique to Croatia, this movement was founded in the 1930s by a group of peasants with no formal artistic education. Their works portray scenes from rural life, employing peculiar perspectives and garish colours.

Museum of Broken Relationships

A few steps away is one of the city's most unusual and compelling attractions, the **Museum of Broken Relationships ⑨** (Muzej prekinutih veza; http://broken ships.com; Jun–Sept 9am–10.30pm, Oct–May 9am–9pm; charge). The humblest objects from around the world tell poignant, witty and often bitter stories of love lost.

St Catherine's Church

At the end of Ćirilometodska is Katarinski trg. Turn left here for **St Catherine's Church ⑩** (Crkva sv. Katarine; free), built by Jesuit monks in the early 17th century, and considered one of the country's most

Museum of Naïve Art work

Lotrščak Tower

beautiful pieces of Baroque architecture. The interior is encrusted with pink-and-white stucco work that resembles icing on a cake. Look out for the extremely deceptive fresco above the altar.

Lotrščak Tower

Cross Katarinski trg, then take the short street of Dverce to **Lotrščak Tower** ⓫ (Kula Lotrščak). Dating back to 1266, this is the best-preserved part of Zagreb's 13th-century fortifications. It originally protected the southern entrance to Gradec, and every evening a bell would ring to signal the closing of the town gates. As the centuries passed, the tower became a firefighters' lookout. These days it is the home of the **Galerija Lotrščak** (Tue–Sun 11am–7pm). Art exhibitions are held here, although many people enter only to climb the tower for a panoramic view of the city.

Every day at noon the **city cannon** is fired from the tower. The tradition began in 1877 when a daily, highly audible 'bang' was considered the best way of synchronising the haphazardly timed chimes of the city's countless church bells. Today, compressed paper and cardboard explode from the barrel with a mighty blast, and children gather below to collect the shreds.

The Lotrščak Tower marks the beginning of **Strossmayer Promenade** (Strossmay-erovo šetalište), which has superb views over Zagreb's rooftops. From here you can take the **funicular** down to Tomićeva for lunch at **Vallis Aurea** (see ❶).

Miraculous Virgin

According to local lore, a terrible fire broke out at the site of the Stone Gate in 1731 and all the surrounding wooden buildings were razed to the ground. Hidden in the ashes: a picture of the Virgin Mary, miracu-lously intact. The Stone Gate thus became a shrine of miracles, where people light a candle and pray. If their prayer is answered they pay tribute to the Virgin with a plaque. Supplication seems to work here: the walls are covered with small marble tab-lets engraved with *hvala* (thank you).

Food and Drink

❶ AÏDA CAFÉ VIENNA

Trg Bana Josipa Jelačića 7; tel: 099-302 0000; daily 8.30am–10.30pm; €

This Zagreb classic makes some of the city's richest cakes, and is one of the favoured morning haunts for coffee and a gossip.

❷ KAVA TAVA

Tkalčićeva 12; tel: 098-1983878; daily 7am–1am; €

Kava Tava is a chilled-out choice for breakfast, brunch, lunch or evening meals. Great people-watching from the terrace.

❸ VALLIS AUREA

Tomićeva 4; tel: 01-483 1305; www.vallis-aurea.com; Mon–Sat 9am–11pm; €€

This cosy restaurant serves up specialities from Slavonia, known for its wine, sausage and hearty paprika-laced dishes.

Trg Nikole šubića Zrinjskog

ZAGREB: LOWER TOWN

This walking tour takes you through the 'green horseshoe', the necklace of parks and gardens that nearly encloses Zagreb's commercial and cultural heart in the Lower Town (Donji grad).

DISTANCE: 3.5km (2.25 miles)
TIME: A half day; a full day with museum visits
START/END: Trg Bana Josipa Jelačića
POINTS TO NOTE: On Mondays most museums are closed. Buy a Zagreb Card to save on admission fees.

Laid out from 1865 to 1887, Zagreb's 'green horseshoe' was intended to bring architecture and greenery into harmony. Most of Zagreb's cultural monuments are displayed along this verdant swathe that runs from the interconnected squares of Trg maršala Tita, Mažuranićev trg and Marulićev trg, across the Botanical Gardens and up the east side from Tomislavov trg, Strossmayerov trg and Zrinjevac to Trg Bana Josipa Jelačića.

TRG BANA JOSIPA JELAČIĆA

If you are starting from the end of route 1, turn left at Ilica and proceed to Oktogon on the right. Otherwise, begin at **Trg Bana Josipa Jelačića ❶**, Zagreb's cen-

tral square that acts as the boundary between the Upper and Lower towns. In the middle of the square stands an imposing statue of *ban* (viceroy) Jelačić upon a horse. Following the orientation of the statue, turn right off the square into Ilica, the city's main shopping street, lined with boutiques.

Stay on the left side of the street and, in about 200m/yds, you will come to the wrought-iron gates of the **Oktogon ❷**, a late 19th-century shopping arcade full of upmarket boutiques and topped by a stained-glass dome.

Trg Petra Preradovića

Pass through the eight-cornered structure and on the other side is **Trg Petra Preradovića ❸**. Petar Preradović (1818–72), after whom the square was named, was a general and Romantic poet. You can see his memorial statue in front of the **Serbian Orthodox Church** (Srpska Pravoslavna Crkva). This square is also called **Cvjetni trg** (Field of the Flowers); it was once the site of a big flower market, although today only a few flower sellers remain.

Trg Bana Josipa Jelačića

National Theatre at night

TRG MARŠALA TITA

From Trg Petra Preradovića, proceed south along Preradovićeva ulica, then take the first right to follow Masarykova to **Trg maršala Tita** ❹ (Marshal Tito Square), the first of a series of three squares that make up one side of the green horseshoe and was laid out by 19th-century Viennese architect Hermann Bollé. The central building here is the neo-Baroque **National Theatre** (Hrvatsko narodno kazalište), completed in a record 14 months in 1895.

In front of the theatre is Ivan Meštrović's enchanting **Well of Life Fountain** (Zdenac života). While still a student in Vienna, the sculptor designed a prototype that featured in an exhibition of works by members of the Vienna Secession movement in 1906. The bronze fountain that you see here was installed in 1912.

On the western side of the square at no. 10 stands the **Museum of Arts and Crafts** ❺ (Muzej za umjetnost i obrt; www.muo.hr; Tue–Sat 10am–7pm, Sun 10am–2pm; charge), also designed by Bollé. Inside is a vast collection of fur-

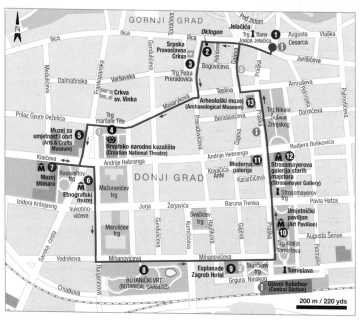

Museum of Arts and Crafts glassware

niture and decorative arts dating from medieval times to the present day. The 17th-century altar of St Mary on the first floor is a standout.

Before leaving the square you could stop for a break at fashionable **Hemingway Bar** (see ❶).

Ethnographic Museum

Proceed south to the adjacent square, Mažuranićev trg, and on your right at no. 14 is the **Ethnographic Museum** ❻ (Etnografski muzej; www.emz.hr; Tue–Fri 10am–6pm, Sat–Sun 10am–1pm; charge).The museum is housed in a monumental 1903 edifice and honours Croatian folk history by showcasing traditional costumes, jewellery and handicrafts. The surprising array of objects from the South Pacific, Asia and South America was amassed by early 20th-century Croatian explorers Mirko and Stevo Seljan.

Mimara Museum

Heading west across the busy Savska cesta, you will come to Rooseveltov trg. Here, at no. 5, a massive grey neo-Renaissance building houses the **Mimara Museum** ❼ (Muzej Mimara; www.mimara. hr; Oct–June Tue–Sat 10am–5pm, Thur until 7pm; July–Sept Tue–Fri 10am–7pm, Sat 10am–5pm, Sun 10am–2pm; charge), containing a somewhat controversial collection of artefacts, including paintings by Flemish and Spanish masters. The museum's founder, Ante Topić Mimara (1898–1987), is something of a mystery, and there are questions over the provenance of his collection. No one has managed to explain the source of his extraordinary wealth.

BOTANICAL GARDENS

Return to Mažuranićev trg, head south to Marulićev trg, then turn left into Mihanovićeva. On the opposite side of the road lie the beautiful **Botanical Gardens** ❽ (Botanički vrt; http://hirc.botanic.hr; daily, check website for opening hours; free), which offer respite from the hustle of the city.

Proceed east along Mihanovićeva to the **Esplanade Zagreb Hotel** ❾ (see page 101). Built in 1925, this illustrious building was originally intended to provide an overnight stop for passengers of the Orient Express, hence the proximity to the **Central Station** (Glavni Kolodvor). You may wish to stop for lunch in the Esplanade's elegant restaurant, **Zinfandel's** (see ❷).

AROUND TRG KRALJA TOMISLAVA

Continue east, passing the equestrian statue of King Tomislav in front of the Central Station. It was Tomislav who drew up a definitive map of Croatian territory in AD925. Turn left on to Praška and the leafy **Trg Kralja Tomislava** (King Tomislav Square) will be on your right. Continue until you reach the **Art Pavilion** ❿ (Umjetnički paviljon; Tues–Thur, Sat–Sun 11am–8pm, Fri 11am–9pm; www.umjetnicki-paviljon.hr; charge) at its centre. The striking yellow Art Nou-

Botanical Gardens bridge *A mix of styles at the Modern Gallery*

veau structure was erected to celebrate '1,000 years of Hungarian Culture' in Budapest in 1896, and now presents changing contemporary art exhibitions.

Modern art and Old Masters

Continue along Praška with **Strossmayerov trg**, another shady park, on your right. On your left is the **Modern Gallery** ⓫ (Moderna galerija; www.moderna-galerija.hr; Tue–Fri 11am–7pm, Sat–Sun 11am–2pm; charge), which is an essential stop for anyone interested in modern Croatian art. All the Croatian masters, from Vlaho Bukovac to Milan Račić, are here.

On your right, housed in the **Croatian Academy of Arts and Sciences**, is the **Strossmayer Gallery of Old Masters** ⓬ (Strossmayerova galerija starih majstora; www.mdc.hr; Tue 10am–1pm and 5–7pm, Wed–Sun 10am–1pm; charge), which represents the collection of Bishop Strossmayer, donated in 1884. The cultivated bishop and advocate for Croatian autonomy amassed works by artists including Bellini, El Greco and Van Dyck.

Archaeological Museum

Continue along Praška to Trg Nikole šubića Zrinjskog, the square at the end of the horseshoe. On your left is the **Archaeological Museum** ⓭ (Arheološki muzej; www.amz.hr; Tue–Sat 10am–6pm, Thur until 8pm, Sat–Sun 10am–1pm; charge). The highlight here is the Egyptian mummy but there are also prehistoric and medieval artefacts, plus one of the largest coin collections in Europe.

Turn left at Teslina and right at Gajeva, where you can eat at **Boban** (see ❸).

Food and Drink

❶ HEMINGWAY BAR

Tuškanac 1; tel: 01-483 4956; www.hemingway.hr; daily 7am–1am; €€
This trendy bar is open all day for coffee and cakes but really takes off at night. Pictures of the 'bearded one' adorn the walls while bartenders mix up Zagreb's most elaborate cocktails. At night smarter attire is expected.

❷ ZINFANDEL'S

Esplanade Zagreb Hotel, Mihanoviçeva 1; tel: 01-456 6644; www.zinfandels.hr; daily 6am–11pm; €€–€€€

A superb hotel deserves a superb restaurant. Chef Ana Grgic fuses contemporary flavours with Balkan specialities to wonderful effect. A lower-priced bistro also offers more casual fare. In either venue, the *štrukli* are a must.

❸ BOBAN

Gajeva 9; tel: 01-481 1549; café open daily 8am–midnight (Sun till 11pm); restaurant open Mon–Thur 11am–11pm, Fri–Sat 11am–midnight; Sun 12–11pm; €
You can eat in the café-lounge-bar upstairs or the downstairs restaurant – or at an outdoor table in nice weather. Choose from the imaginative Italian menu, and be prepared to wait.

Brooding statue of Tito in Staro Selo

ZAGORJE

Escape from the bustle of Zagreb to the hills of Zagorje, which lie to the north of the capital. This is a land of farmhouses, castles and medieval fortresses, with Staro Selo – the birthplace of Tito and now a fascinating open-air ethnographic museum – a star attraction.

DISTANCE: 170km (106 miles)
TIME: A full day
START/END: Zagreb
POINTS TO NOTE: This itinerary requires a car, as neither Veliki Tabor nor Trakošćan can be reached by public transport (although it is possible to do a half-day trip from Zagreb to Kumrovec by local train, changing at Savski Marof). Make an early start, and time it to arrive in Grešna Gorica for lunch.

The undulating farmland, vineyards and rural villages of the Croatian hinterland, **Zagorje**, are less than an hour north of Zagreb. Unlike the Mediterranean style of the coast, the cool hills, hearty cuisine and German-speaking inhabitants feel distinctly Central European.

To get to the region, leave Zagreb via Zagorska magistrala (Route 225), the former main road to Ljubljana, which runs parallel to the E59/A2 motorway. Although not the quickest route, it is the more interesting one.

INTO THE HILLS

After driving for approximately 15km (10 miles), head west to Luka then head north. Another 5km (3.25 miles) along you will pass through the village of **Veliko Trgovišće ❶**, the birthplace of the late President Tuđman. You cannot miss the house: a single-storey, green-and-white affair on the corner, to your right, with a chequered Croatian flag in the garden and a memorial plaque. Tuđman, it seems, hoped to be immortalised in the way Tito was.

After Veliko Trgovišće take a route north through the rolling hills until you reach Route 205. Note the vineyards planted in narrow strips running vertically down the slopes, each with its own small wooden hut *(klet)*, that was traditionally used for storing wine.

Villages in the area like Družilovec and Dubrovčan are typical rural settlements with steep tiled roofs, open-sided wooden barns filled with maize, and ducks and geese waddling along the roadside.

Farm buildings at Staro Selo

KLANJEC

Once on Route 205 travel west until you reach **Klanjec** ❷ on the River Sutla. Although dominated by the imposing **Franciscan Monastery**, Klanjec is most notable as the birthplace of the sculptor Antun Augustinčić (1900–79), who created the *Monument to Peace* in front of the United Nations headquarters in New York. In the centre of town is the **Galerija** (www.mdc.

hr/augustincic/hr/home.html; Apr–Sept daily 9am–5pm, Oct–Mar Tue–Sun 9am–3pm; charge), a modern museum with a striking collection of works by this remarkable artist. Notice especially the drawings and photos tracing the artistic development of the *Monument to Peace*.

STARO SELO

Continue northwest along the River Sutla for 6km (4 miles) to **Kumrovec**, the childhood home of the Yugoslav president Josip Broz Tito. The centre of the village has been turned into the open-air ethnological museum of **Staro Selo** ❸ (www.mdc.hr/kumrovec/hr/index.html; Apr–Sept daily 9am–7pm, Oct–Mar 9am–4pm; charge). Meaning Old Village, Staro Selo comprises 20 carefully restored thatched cottages and a dozen wooden farm buildings devoted to local handicrafts and traditions. There's a blacksmith, a potter and even a gingerbread-maker, and every Sunday from May to September, visiting craftsmen give demonstrations. The simple dwellings, clustered around the stream and set amid lovingly tended gardens and orchards, paint an idealised picture of 19th-century rural life.

There's no doubt about which is Tito's house; a life-size statue of the man (by Augustinčić) stands in the garden. Inside, it is arranged as it would have been when Tito was a boy, with

Fortress of Veliki Tabor

simple furniture and a kitchen blackened by soot from smoking hams. People still live within the complex, but the village is more animated by farm animals. You can buy a traditional *licitarsko srce* (gingerbread heart) at the souvenir shop, and there is a small café on site.

Miljana

On leaving Kumrovec, drive north through Zagorska Sela and Plavić. Again the road runs parallel with the River Sutla to your left, and fields and woodland to your right. You will eventually reach the 17th-century manor of **Miljana** ❹. Although it is private property, you can drive up to the gate to better admire the majestic Baroque exterior. Turn right here for Veliki Tabor and Desinić.

Hilltop castle of Trakošćan

VELIKI TABOR

You will see the impressive fortress of **Veliki Tabor** ❺ (www.veliki-tabor. hr; Apr–Sept Tue–Fri 9am–5pm, Sat–Sun 9am–7pm, Oct–Mar Tue–Fri 9am–4pm, Sat–Sun 9am–5pm; charge) perched on a hilltop just before the village of Desinić long before you arrive. Turn left, follow the track and park in front of the main gate. This is one of the area's best-preserved castles. The central core, a pentagonal tower, was built in the 12th century. The semi-circular towers were added in the 15th and 16th centuries as protection against the Turks. Unfortunately, the exhibits inside – collections of tools, period weaponry, household and religious objects, paintings and pottery – fail to do justice to the imposing turrets and towers.

After exploring the fortress, return to the main road and turn left for **Desinić**. Within a kilometre, you will see a sign to the right that reads '**Grešna Gorica**' (see ❶). This is a good place to stop for lunch.

TRAKOŠĆAN CASTLE

Try to finish lunch by 2.30pm, as you will need at least an hour to reach the castle at Trakošćan. Head east via Pregrada to Krapina (20km/12.5 miles). At Krapina, head north on to the E59 motorway until you reach the turning east for **Trakošćan** ❻ (www.

Veliki Tabor archways   *Boating lake at Trakošćan*

trakoscan.hr; daily Apr–Oct 9am–6pm, Nov–Mar 9am–4pm; charge), a splendid hilltop castle. Below are a car park, gift shop and bar.

The castle as it is seen today dates largely from the 19th century. In 1569, the small fortress that had been here for centuries, and its estate, were taken by the Royal Treasury and granted to the Bishop of Zagreb and Viceroy of Croatia, Juraj Drašković. The bishop treated the peasantry badly, and after four years they rebelled. Their ringleader, Matija Gubec, was arrested and Drašković had him 'crowned with molten iron for his impertinence'. The bishop handed Trakošćan on to his brother, and it remained in the Drašković family until 1944, when they emigrated to Austria and the property was nationalised.

The building was uninhabited from the 16th to the 19th centuries. Towards the end of this period, when the German Romantic movement was fashionable among Central European aristocrats, Trakošćan suddenly became popular. No longer a defence post, but a fairy-tale castle in the wilderness, the building was remodelled in neo-Gothic style, and the grounds landscaped on the model of an English park. A dam was built, and the valley turned into an artificial lake.

However, the original interior is still intact. The dark, heavy wooden furniture is complemented by solemn family portraits, many painted by Julijana

Drašković (1847–1901).

End your visit with a walk by the lake (full circuit, 6km/4 miles) and a drink at the floating bar, **Terasa na Jezeru** (May–Sept) on a raft. Although the floating bar is open only during the summer season, there is a café opposite that is open during the winter as well. Return to Zagreb on the E59.

While driving, you may notice houses painted an unusual turquoise-blue colour. In the past, to protect the grapes from pests, vines were sprayed with a solution of blue copper crystals known as 'Bordeaux juice'. Any solution left over was used to paint the houses. It kept flies away during the summer months, although it is also believed to have had a detrimental effect on locals' health.

Food and Drink

① GREŠNA GORICA

Desinić; tel: 049-343 001; www.gresna-gorica.com; daily 10am–10pm; €
Everything on the menu here is homemade, and all the ingredients are supplied by local farmers. Besides the hearty meat dishes that are typical of Zagorje and feature duck, pork and local venison, you might want to try *zagorski štrukli*, a sort of maize dumpling served with fresh curd cheese. There is lots of space around this rustic restaurant, plus a playground and farmhouse zoo.

An electric ferry crosses Kozjak

PLITVICE LAKES NATIONAL PARK

A chance to explore the lakes, waterfalls and forests of Plitvice Lakes National Park. Just off the main road from Zagreb to Split, Plitvice can be visited as a day trip from the capital, or en route between the two cities (there are three hotels for overnight stays).

DISTANCE: 10km (6.25 miles), including shuttle and boat trip
TIME: A half day
START: Entrance 2
END: Entrance 1
POINTS TO NOTE: Plitvice is at its most beautiful in spring, when snowmelt increases the water volume, and in autumn. In winter, local roads are occasionally blocked with snow; the lakes and falls may freeze, and, although the park is stunning, few of its facilities are operating.

To reach the park from Zagreb (167km/ 104 miles; about two hours), take the motorway A1 to the Cvor Bjelolasica exit and take Route 42 south. Alternatively, there are about 13 buses a day between Zagreb bus station (www.akz.hr) and the coast that stop at both park entrances on request; be sure the driver knows in advance where you want to get off.

The route described is just one possible way to approach the park. Walks of different lengths are signposted from both entrances. If you wish to see the dramatic Veliki Slap first, start from Entrance 1.

Croatia's oldest and largest national park, **Plitvice Lakes** (Plitvička jezera; www.np-plitvicka-jezera.hr; daily 8am–6pm; charge) is the country's most visited inland destination, attracting up to 1.2 million visitors a day. Due to its outstanding natural beauty, it was proclaimed a Unesco World Heritage Site in 1979. Plitvice is a lovely place for walking, with a network of trails skirting the shores of the lakes and wooden footpaths crisscrossing the cascades.

A unique landscape

The park encompasses a succession of 16 lakes (*jezera*) linked by a series of spectacular waterfalls (*slapovi*). These were formed by a geological process that has been going on for thousands of years and is still taking place today. When water flows over limestone, it picks up and then deposits calcium carbonate that encrusts algae and moss to form natural travertine barriers and dams. These, in turn, create lakes and cascades.

Hiking in the Upper Lakes

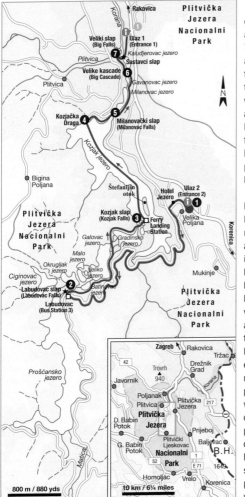

The park is densely forested with beech, as well as fir on land lying above 700m (2,300ft). The trees are vital to the ecosystem: without their roots the ground soil would be washed away. Also here are laurel, elderberry, holly, honeysuckle and ferns, plus orchids, lilies, hyacinths, cyclamen and peonies, many protected by law.

Swimming, fishing and hunting are prohibited, but if you are lucky you may spot one of the wild animals that live here, including deer, otters, badgers, lynx and wild boar, plus about 50 brown bears (the symbol of Plitvice). Packs of wolves also roam the area in winter. Birdwatchers should look out for woodpeckers and black stork, plus rare golden eagles and peregrine falcons in the woods, and grey herons, white-throated dippers and black-throated divers close to the water. For their part, the lakes support trout and chub, plus countless ducks and water snakes.

Path through the Upper Lakes

THE UPPER LAKES

There are two entrances to Plitvice: start your tour from **Entrance 2** ❶, close to the upper end of the system of lakes and cascades, to follow the course of the water downriver to Entrance 1. If you are arriving from Zagreb, pass Entrance 1 and proceed to Entrance 2 at **Velika Poljana**, where you will find a large car park on the left-hand side of the road, plus a cluster of wooden chalets that house an information centre, a general store, an office dealing in private accommodation and a café.

From the car park, a wooden footbridge rises above the main road, bringing you to a footpath on the other side, which leads through the trees to **Hotel Jezero** (see page 101). Behind the hotel, the path takes you past **Buffet Flora**, where you might stop for a drink, to a wooden hut selling entrance tickets.

From here, national park shuttle buses (price included in entrance fee) make regular runs to various locations in the park. Take a bus to **Station 3** at **Labudovac**, close to the first and highest lake, **Prošćansko** (639m/2,096ft above sea level).

Down to Goat's Lake

At Labudovac, turn right and follow the path downhill. The first lake that you will see on your left is **Okrugljak** ❷, site of a large cave topped with travertine 'curtains'. The next big lake down is **Galovac**, where the travertine has created a series of falls of exceptional beauty. Cross over the lake at the bottom and continue on the path alongside a succession of lakes downstream to **Kozjak Falls** ❸, which run into the largest lake, **Kozjak** (Kozjak jezero means Goat's Lake). According to local legend, Kozjak earned its name after a herd of goats (*koza* means goat in Croatian) drowned here when crossing thin ice while trying to escape from wolves one winter. Most of the Plitvice lakes are named after people or things that have disappeared in them: Ciginovac was apparently named after a gypsy (*cigan*) who drowned in it while fishing, while Gavanovac was named after a rich man (*gavan*) who lost a hoard of treasure there.

Close to Kozjak Falls lies a **Landing Station**. Hop aboard the national park electric ferry (summer every 10 minutes, winter every 30 minutes; price included in entrance fee) for a 20-minute ride across the lake, passing by **Štefanija's Island** (Štefanijin otok). This is named after Princess Stefanie of Belgium, who married into the Habsburg family in the late 19th century – when Croatia was under Habsburg rule – and visited Plitvice in 1888.

THE LOWER LAKES

The boat journey ends at the north end of the lake, at **Kozjačka Draga** ❹,

Veliki Slap   *Velike Kascade*

where you will find a leafy glade with a snack bar, picnic area and wooden kiosks selling local produce throughout the summer. From here, turn right to follow the water, which has by now taken on a brilliant emerald colour (due to the high mineral content of the limestone bedrock and the light) through the *Korana Canyon*.

Veliki Slap

Take the wooden walkway over **Milanovac Falls** ❺ and follow the path alongside the eastern side of the small lakes of **Milanovac** and **Gavanovac**. Cross over **Velike Kascade** ❻ (Big Cascades) to walk alongside **Kaludjerovac**, then turn left to **Veliki Slap** ❼ (Big Falls). Veliki Slap, the park's highest and most dramatic waterfall (78m/256ft), is supplied by water from a separate source, the River Plitvica. Wedding ceremonies are held in certain parts of the park, particularly underneath Veliki Slap.

From here, all the waters meet to flow into the last and lowest lake, **Novakovića Brod** (503m/1,650ft above sea level), and form the River Korana, which flows through a steep-sided rocky canyon to Karlovac, where it meets the River Kupa. It then proceeds to join first the River Sava then the Danube and flows east through Romania to empty eventually into the Black Sea.

Leave Veliki Slap by taking the wooden walkway that crosses the water just above **Sastavci Falls** (Sastavci slap), then follow the steep and serpentine footpath uphill to **Entrance 1** at the northern end of the park. Here you will find a small general store selling basic foodstuffs and national park souvenirs, as well as **Lička Kuća** restaurant (see ❶).

Alternatively, from Entrance 1, you can walk via a signposted path, or take a national park shuttle bus, back to Entrance 2 where you began.

Food and Drink

❶ LIČKA KUĆA

Entrance 1; Rastovača bb;
tel: 053-751 382; daily 11am–10pm;
€€

Plitvice is in the Lika region, which is known for its hearty, rustic fare. Although touristy, this restaurant remains an excellent place to sample local favourites such as *lička juha*, a heavy soup consisting of lamb, vegetables, lemon and sour cream and *pladanj lička*, a mixed platter of meat and potatoes prepared under a *peka*, a cast-iron bell that is covered with hot embers and cooks the food slowly. If you do not eat meat, opt for trout, cheese and salad. As you wait for your meal, try a glass of potent *šljivovica* (plum brandy). The mock rustic interior and large open fire create a cosy and comfortable ambience.

Attractive Rovinj

ISTRIAN COAST

Spend a day exploring the rugged Istrian coast. After a look at the Roman ruins of Pula, enjoy a seafood lunch at the Lim Channel, then proceed to the Byzantine mosaics of St Euphrasius' Basilica in Poreč. End the day with sunset cocktails and dinner in Rovinj.

DISTANCE: 130km (81 miles)
TIME: A full day
START/END: Pula
POINTS TO NOTE: To get the most out of this trip you need a car, although it is possible to follow the route from Pula to Poreč and on to Rovinj by bus. Local tourist offices (see page 129) should be able to advise on bus schedules. Make an early start, and bring comfortable shoes and a swimming costume.

Istria (Istra) takes its name from the first settlers here, the Illyrian tribe of the Histri. When the Romans conquered the peninsula in the 2nd century BC, they built fortified military towns on the former Histri settlements. The most important of these were Parentium (Poreč) and Pola (Pula).

Istria has always had close ties with Italy. From 1918 to 1945, following the collapse of the Habsburg Empire, it was subject to Italian sovereignty. Then, at the end of World War II, the territory was incorporated into Yugoslavia, although the Italian population was still recognised as a minority group, with its own schools and media, funded in part by the Italian government. Many Istrian towns and villages still have both Croatian and Italian names.

The rugged Istrian coastline is not so blessed with beaches as southern Croatia, but the cultural attractions here more than make up for it. Plus, there's a particularly agreeable 'Istrian' way of life that includes taking great pride in their local heritage, a devotion to good cuisine and a welcoming live-and-let-live attitude. For a tour of inland Istria, see route 6 (see page 50).

PULA

On the southern tip of the Istrian peninsula is **Pula ❶**, still the region's largest and most important city, just as it was 2,000 years ago when the Romans chose it as their administrative base. In addition to tourism, shipbuilding at Pula's Uljanik shipyard remains central to the local economy.

Pula's Arena

Roman relics

In the centre of town you will find the monumental 1st century Roman amphitheatre, known as the **Arena** (daily Jan–Mar, Nov–Dec 9am–5pm, Apr 8am–8pm, May–June, Sept 8am–9pm, July–Aug 8am–12am, Oct 9am–7pm; charge). This three-storey oval structure was designed to seat 23,000 spectators and is the sixth-largest surviving building of its kind in the world. During the 16th century, the Venetians carried off a good number of Istria's Roman relics, and it seems that they even considered dismantling the arena and rebuilding it in Venice. Today the ancient amphitheatre – whose exterior is still remarkably intact – plays host to a lively programme of summer festivals and rock concerts.

Cross Flavijevska and the small park to arrive at Riva, the seafront promenade. Turn left, passing the harbour and yacht marina, to arrive at the **Cathedral** (Katedrala; summer daily 7am–noon and 4–6pm, winter Mass only; free), which started as a 5th-century basilica, built on the foundations of a Roman temple. Its 17th-century bell tower was built of stone taken from the arena.

On the other side of the cathedral, follow Kandlerova to arrive at the Forum, today Pula's main square and once, as the name indicates, the Roman forum. Note the well-preserved **Temple of Augustus** that stands next to the 13th-century Town Hall (Gradska vijećnica). From the Forum, take traffic-free **Sergijevaca** on the southeast corner to arrive at the imposing **Sergius Arch** (also known as Zlatna Vrata – Golden Gate), which was erected in 27 BC.

Close by stands the house in which Irish writer James Joyce lived for a brief period in 1904–5 when he worked as an English teacher at the Berlitz School. In the same building is the pleasant **Caffè Uliks** (Ulysses; see ❶).

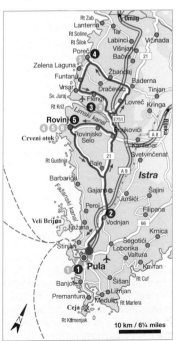

Lim Channel

LIM CHANNEL

From Pula heading north, take Route 3 passing **Vodnjan** ❷ and Bale (22km/ 13.5 miles). En route you will see several *kažuni*, small circular stone structures peculiar to Istria, built by local farmers. A few kilometres after Brajkovići, a sign saying 'Limski kanal' will direct you to the left. Follow the road downhill to the parking lot for the **Lim Channel** ❸ (Limski kanal; also known as Lim Fjord or Limska Draga Fjord). Lined by steep forested walls, the 10km (6-mile) fjord is one of Istria's most dramatic sights. The clean, pure water has made the fjord a prime spot for farmed mussels and oysters; two of Istria's best seafood restaurants are located here. This is a good place to stop for a swim and a seafood lunch at either **Restaurant Viking** (see ❷) or **Fjord**.

POREČ

After lunch, return to the main road and head north. Head past Lovreč to Baderna and then take Route 302 west to **Poreč** ❹ (about 25km/16 miles). The historic town centre is a fascinating place to wander, and still bears traces of Poreč's many occupiers, from the Romans to the Byzantines and the Venetians. A network of seaside resorts stretches north and south of town, making Poreč a busy place at the height of summer.

Leave your car in the large waterfront car park and take the coastal prome-nade, **Nikole Tesle**, into the Old Town. You will quickly arrive at **Trg Slobode**, a large square lined with cafés.

City Museum

The cobbled street that veers off to your right is **Decumanus**, which forms a central axis the length of the Old Town. The straight streets follow the original Roman plan, while the elegant building façades are clearly Venetian inspired. Follow Decumanus a few blocks and on the left at no. 9 you will see the Baroque Sinčić Palace, which is home to the **City Museum** (Gradski muzej; summer 10am–1pm and 6–9pm, winter 10am– noon; charge). It contains prehistoric pottery, fragments of Roman sculpture and portraits of local notables.

Basilica of St Euphrasius

Continue south on Decumanus a short way until you see a sign to the right, 'Bazilika', which brings you directly into the 6th-century atrium of the **Basilica of St Euphrasius** (Eufrazijeva bazilika; July–Aug 9am–9pm, Apr–June, Sept–Oct 9am–6pm, Nov–Dec Mon– Sat 9am–4pm; charge). What started as a little oratory in the 4th century grew to become a basilica in the 5th century. In the 6th century, Bishop Euphrasius expanded it into a complex that included an episcopal palace, an atrium, a baptistery and a chapel. Adopting the lavish style of Byzantium's 'Golden Age', all the buildings were ornamented with mosaics. Much of the

St Euphrasius mosaic   *Poreč viewed from the bell tower*

original architecture and nearly all the mosaics remain intact.

The silence and simplicity of the interior – rough tiled floor, bare walls and sturdy columns with discreet ornamentation – produce a reverential atmosphere in this Unesco-protected treasure. Be sure to look at the splendid golden mosaics in the apse, which were created by craftsmen from Constantinople and Ravenna.

On the opposite side of the atrium stands the baptistery, presided over by a 16th-century **bell tower**. Climb to the top for magnificent views; on a fine day you might even see Venice.

Go back to Decumanus and continue to **Trg Matije Gupca**, a square with a raised garden and benches where locals gather to exchange news in the shade of the trees. Keep on the main axis and to the left you will see the 13th-century **Romanesque House** (Romanička kuća) with a well-preserved wooden balcony.

Temples and monuments

On the tip of the peninsula lies **Trg Marafor**, the forum in Roman times, and site of two ancient temples. In the park at the end of the square stand fragments of the **Temple of Neptune**, built in the 2nd century to honour the god of the sea. Too little remains of the other temple to identify it.

Along the southern side of the peninsula runs **Obala maršala Tita**. The town's oldest hotels look out over the harbour from here, and there are numerous boats to and from the island of **Sveti Nikola** (a one-hour return trip), which is the area's best place for bathing. You can also see two well-kept monuments bearing the Red Star to commemorate those Croats and Italians who opposed Fascism during World War II – a rare sight in Croatia today.

Stop off at **Hitri** (see ③) if you are feeling hungry, then leave Poreč by car, taking the coastal road south past the tourist complexes of Plava Laguna and Zelena Laguna. Drive through Funtana – named after the freshwater springs the Romans used to supply their summer villas – and then turn left before the town of **Vrsar**, home of **Koversada**, the renowned naturist camp. The road now turns inland and passes through the villages of Flengi and Kloštar.

ROVINJ

At the village of Brajkovići, turn right, passing through Rovinjsko Selo, to arrive in **Rovinj** ➎. The town, founded on an island, was fortified during the Middle Ages. In the 18th century, the narrow channel separating it from the mainland was filled, and urban development extended beyond the walls. Thus the Old Town, confined to a small peninsula presided over by a hilltop cathedral, remains unspoilt: indeed, it is possibly Istria's most attractive port town. The many centuries that Rovinj spent under Venetian rule are evident in the Venetian-Gothic windows and the St

Rovinj harbour

Mark lion motif that crops up throughout the town.

Park along the waterfront and then follow **Obala palih boraca** to the town centre. You will soon arrive at **Trg maršala Tita**. Amid the tourist hubbub, there is still one decent café: **Viecia Batana** (see ❹), at no. 8, is an atmospheric place to stop for a rest.

Rovinj Museum

At the northern end of the square is the **Rovinj Museum** (Zavičajni musej Rovinj; www.muzej-rovinj.com; summer Tue–Sat 10am–1pm; charge), with halls devoted to Old Masters such as the Renaissance artists Giovanni Bellini and Bonifazio de Pitati and Baroque artists Marco Ricci, Antonio Zanchi, Girolamo Romanino and Nicolò Grassi. Local and contemporary Croatian artists are also represented, and there is an archaeological collection.

Cathedral of St Euphemia

A few steps further north, pass through the 17th-century Baroque **Balbi's Arch** (Balbijev luk). From here take any of the narrow cobbled streets that climb towards the hilltop **Cathedral of St Euphemia** (Katedrala sv. Eufenija; summer 10am–6pm, winter variable hours; free). Modelled after the St Mark's bell tower in Venice, the 60m (197ft) high Baroque tower is perhaps Rovinj's most defining feature. The remains of St Euphemia, who was martyred during the reign of Emperor Diocletian (AD245–312), are said to lie in a sar-

cophagus inside the cathedral. According to legend, the casket floated out to sea from Constantinople, and was washed ashore here in AD800.

Seafront sunset

Return to town by taking the stepped street of **Grisia**, which becomes an open-air art gallery every year on a Sunday in August. From Trg maršala Tita turn right on to Obala Pina Budicina and stroll along the quay with the rest of the early evening crowd. You will shortly come to **Sv. Križa**, an excellent vantage point to watch the sunset. The best place to view the show is from **Mediterraneo Bar** (see ❺). For dinner you could stop at the nearby **Konoba Veli Jože** (see ❻) to sample Istrian specialities.

To return to Pula (32km/20 miles), head south, passing through the small settlement of Spanidiga, following signs to Bale. Once you reach Bale, turn right towards Vodnjan and then on to Pula.

Active Rovinj

Within easy reach of Rovinj's hilly Old Town is a wealth of opportunities for active travellers. Just a short boat ride away (every half-hour from the boat dock in front of Trg maršala Tita) is Crveni otok (Red Island), a summer favourite for its numerous swimming coves, some of which are reserved for naturists. The crystal waters off Rovinj are a magnet for scuba-divers, especially those wishing to explore the wreck of the *Baron Gautsch*, an Austrian ocean liner sunk

Old Town charm   *Boat trip to Red Island*

in 1914. The wreck is off limits except for divers in organised groups. You can organise a dive through Mediterraneum Mare Sport in Villas Rubin, 3km (1.8 miles) from Rovinj's centre (052-816 648; www.mmsport.hr).

Back on land is Zlatni Rt-Punta Corrente, a magnificent protected forest on the southern side of Rovinj. Cypresses, Douglas firs, cedars and stone pines offer shade for a refreshing stroll along the landscaped promenades. Too sedate? Go vertical. A Venetian quarry on the park's seaside has dozens of rock-climbing routes, suitable for all levels. Also near Rovinj, 8km (5 miles) to the southwest, is the Palud swamp (Jan–Oct daily 8am–9pm; charge), Istria's only ornithological reserve, which is home to more than 200 bird species.

Food and Drink

① ULIKS

Trg Portorata I, Pula; tel: 052-219 158; daily 6am–2am; €

A sculpture of James Joyce reminds you that this café was one of his favourite haunts. It remains immensely popular with locals and visitors, mostly because of its superb location.

② RESTAURANT VIKING

Lim Channel; tel: 052-448 223; daily 11am–11pm; €€

Sample Lim seafood at Viking, which is situated right on the waterfront with a large terrace. Try the oysters on ice, noodles with scampi and porcini mushrooms, or baked fish with potatoes.

③ HITRI

Eufrazijeva 7, Poreč; tel: 095-546 5515; daily 5pm–1am; €

This lively restaurant serves Mediterranean specialities, although the giant meat platters could be enough.

④ VIECIA BATANA

Trg maršala Tita 8, Rovinj; daily 8am–10pm; €

Especially popular with locals for morning coffee, this café overlooks the harbour and offers a perfect vantage point to observe the comings and goings of boats, especially during annual regattas. Good cakes and ice cream are served too.

⑤ MEDITERRANEO BAR

Sv. Križa 21, Rovinj; tel: 091-532 8357; daily noon–midnight; €

Just sit on the terrace, drink in hand, and gaze at the sea as it changes colours while the sun sets.

⑥ KONOBA VELI JOŽE

Sv. Križa 1; tel: 052-816 337; daily 11am–1am; €€

Here you can taste old-fashioned Istrian fare such as *fuži* (pasta) with goulash and *bakalar na bijelo* (salt-cod pâté).

Pazin Castle and Abyss

HEART OF ISTRIA

Overlooked by many tourists, the rolling countryside of inland Istria offers such treasures as the dramatic abyss at Pazin, remarkable frescoes at Beram and the stunning hill towns of Motovun and Grožnjan. You can also stop off at Hum, self-proclaimed 'world's smallest town'.

DISTANCE: 100km (62 miles)
TIME: One or two days
START/END: Pazin
POINTS TO NOTE: This itinerary is designed as a round trip from Pazin and requires a car, which can easily be hired in tourist centres on the coast if that is where you are based. If you are restricted to public transport, you can still cover part of the route: take a local bus from Pazin to Motovun and a local bus or train from Pazin to Buzet. If you wish to spend two days doing this tour, consider staying overnight in Motovun.

Numerous visitors to Istria (Istra) head straight for the coast, but the region most cherished by the majority of Croatians is **Srce Istre** (Heart of Istria). This inland terrain of hills and valleys, planted with woods and vineyards, is best known for the romantic silhouettes of its hill towns. While Pazin and eastern Istria were, for several hundred years, ruled by Austria, the area west of Pazin was answerable to Venice. The two regions were united in

1805, as one of Napoleon's many geographical revisions.

PAZIN

The tour begins at **Pazin ❶**, inland Istria's largest town, which for centuries was known by its German name, Mitterburg (Central Town). The name is fitting for a town right in the centre of Istria that is neither large nor small, neither ancient nor modern, neither prosperous nor poor. Pazin is a pleasant and easy-going town unused to seeing much tourism, which in itself makes it worth a visit. It does mean, however, that if you stay in Pazin, you should be aware that there are no notable restaurants in town. Just 7km (5 miles) southeast out of town, however, is the homespun food of **Marino** (see ❶).

Pazin Abyss

The settlement developed around a castle built above a dramatic gorge, the **Pazin Abyss** (Pazinska Jama). The 100m (330ft) deep chasm is a natural phenomenon formed by the River Paz-

'Dance Macabre' in Beram's Church of St Mary

inčića, which flows into a semi-circular cave called, appropriately enough, Dante's lobby. A series of lakes and subterranean canals siphons the flow into a network of streams and tributaries under the porous rock. One large underground lake is directly beneath the castle, but the thickly forested terrain blocks a view of the entrance.

The seemingly bottomless pit set the French author Jules Verne wondering if it leads to the Lim Channel (see page 46). It most likely does not, but that did not stop Verne from writing *Mathias Sandorf* (1885), where the novel's hero jumps into the Pazin Abyss and emerges in the Lim Channel.

Pazin Castle

A stroll around the well-maintained castle perched on a cliff over the abyss makes it easy to imagine such improbable adventures. The castle houses the **Ethnographic Museum of Istria** (Etnografski muzej Istre; www.emi.hr; Tue–Thur 10am–3pm, Fri 11am–4pm, Sat–Sun 10am–4pm; charge), with well-displayed collections of traditional costumes, farm implements and the like. Also here is the **Civic Museum of Pazin** (Gradski muzej). During the summer, concerts are held in the courtyard, and there is a week of festivities in mid-June celebrating Jules Verne.

BERAM

From Pazin take the main road west for Poreč. After 5km (3 miles), take the narrow road to the right leading up a hill to **Beram ②**. This site was first settled by the Illyrians as a prehistoric hill fort (*gradina*) and later became a fortified medieval town. Now a sleepy village, Beram wakes up once a year, when local farmers bring wine here to be blessed on **St Martin's Day**, which is 11 November. A 'bishop' blesses the must (fermenting grape juice), warning that it is a sin to make *delanec* (wine fortified with added sugar, diluted with water or abused in any other way). After this ritual, the townsfolk tuck into a feast

Hilltop Motovun

of roast goose and *mlinci* (baked noodles) plus, of course, an endless flow of local wine.

Beram's frescoes

The main reason to visit Beram, however, is to see the extraordinary 15th-century frescoes in the **Church of St Mary** (Crkva sv. Marija na Škriljinah). The interior walls are entirely covered with a vivid and colourful cycle of frescoes that date from 1474. Over time they were hidden by mortar and whitewashed, only to be rediscovered and restored in 1913. Painted by local artist Vincent of Kastav and his assistants, these frescoes were not only decorative, but also served as a 'Bible for the Illiterate'. The biblical scenes depicted were intended to educate and amuse the congregation. The frescoes feature a backdrop of 15th-century Istrian countryside, thereby giving us a fascinating record of life in those times. The most notable piece is the allegorical *Danse Macabre* above the main door. Detailed explanations in English are available. The church is kept locked: either phone the church custodian (tel: 052-626 026) or the key-holder (tel: 052-622 903) about half an hour before you arrive in Beram. Together you will drive the kilometre or so to the church.

MOTOVUN

From Beram proceed north 16km (10 miles) to **Motovun** ❸. As you navigate the treacherous hairpin bends, you may find it of interest to know that the eminent American racing driver Mario Andretti (Formula 1 world champion in 1978) was born in these parts in 1940. The town is also known for its annual five-day **Motovun Film Festival** (late July–early Aug; www.motovunfilm festival.com), during which a giant campsite is set up at the foot of the village.

The car park (charge) is about 100m/yds before the entrance to the town. Take the cobbled street uphill to arrive at the first town gate, built at the beginning of the 14th century and adorned with reliefs of Venetian lions. Further uphill, the second gate leads to Motovun's main square, which is dominated by the 17th-century **Church of St Stephen** (Crkva sv. Stjepan). Built according to plans by one of the founding fathers of Renaissance architecture, Andrea Palladio, this Renaissance-Baroque jewel harbours several treasures. Note the 17th-century painting of *The Last Supper* behind the main altar and the 18th-century ceiling paintings. Next to the church is the 13th-century Gothic **bell tower** that looms over the town.

Across from the church is the Renaissance **Municipal Palace** and annexes (closed to the public), built between the 14th and 19th centuries. The medieval well in front of the church dates from the 14th century, when the town drew water from the cistern underneath the town square.

Grožnjan hues   *Grožnjan – 'City of Artists'*

Town walls

Just outside the second gate is the **Hotel Kaštel** (see ❷), with a large shady terrace; it is an inviting place for refreshment, as well as a comfortable place to stay the night. A path at the far side of the town square leads to a promenade along the 13th-century town walls, from which there are splendid views of the surrounding valley. The terrain is neatly crisscrossed by vineyards that produce the excellent Teran red wine. It takes only about 15 minutes to make a circuit of the walls, and you will see that the town is divided into three parts: the nucleus of the Old Town which you have just left, a suburb on the southern slope of the hill and a more modern residential development on the eastern ridge.

GROŽNJAN

When leaving Motovun, turn right at the bottom of the hill and, about 4km (3 miles) later, turn left in the direction of Buje to the west. A few kilometres after the roundabout in the tiny hamlet of Ponte Porton there's a sign on the right for **Grožnjan ❹**. Ignore that sign (which leads to an unsurfaced and tortuous road), and turn right at the second sign a few kilometres later. A winding but paved road takes you right up to Grožnjan (called Grisignana in Italian).

Artists' colony

This medieval fortified town, historically and architecturally similar to Motovun, is now a haven of art and music. For years it was ignored and neglected until, in 1965, the local council proclaimed Grožnjan a 'City of Artists'. Painters, sculptors and potters were invited to set up their workshops here on the condition that they carried out restoration work on the dilapidated stone buildings. Consequently, Grožnjan is now home to more than 40 small galleries and studios.

Every summer, from June to September, the Hrvatska Glazbena Mladež organisation (International Federation of Musical Youth) runs a summer school in Grožnjan. In the morning the cobbled streets reverberate with the tuning of stringed instruments, and evenings culminate with a lively programme of concerts.

For lunch, you could go to **Konoba Bastija** (see ❸). Alternatively, stop in Livade (first turning on the left on the road between Grožnjan and Buzet) at the award-winning **Zigante** (see ❹), specialising in truffles.

TOWARDS HUM

When leaving Grožnjan, double back and turn left along the scenic main road in the direction of Buzet, 21km (13 miles) to the east. You are now passing through the valley of the **River Mirna**, an area renowned for truffles. Indeed, the biggest truffle in the world was unearthed here in 1999 by Giancarlo Gigante. Throughout the month of October, truffle festivals are a major attraction here. On the agenda are truffle-tasting sessions and demon-

Hum, small but perfectly formed

strations of the way in which dogs are used to unearth this prized delicacy.

Glagolitic Alley

Pass Buzet and pass the first sign to Pazin. Turn right at the second sign to Pazin and continue until a sign directs you to Hum. Now turn right to take the **Glagolitic Alley ⑤** (Aleja glagoljaša), leading to Hum. Glagolitic Alley is a 7km (4-mile) stretch of road that features 11 sculptural compositions erected in the 1970s to commemorate people and events connected with the Glagolitic script. The script was a form of writing thought to have been invented by Saint Cyril in Constantinople in the 9th century. It was used by the Old Slavonic Church in the Balkans until the 10th century, when Cyrillic (also invented by Saint Cyril) became established in Serbia, Bulgaria and Russia. In the face of opposition from the Vatican, Glagolitic remained the dominant alphabet in Croatia until the 14th century. The Roman script then took over, due to the influence of Croatian scholars who had studied in Italy. The most renowned Glagolitic record is a stone tablet dating from the 12th century, known as the Baška Ploča; there are more replicas of Glagolitic works in front of a small church near the village of Brnobići.

HUM

Hum ⑥ claims to be the smallest town in the world. Fewer than two dozen people live here, but Mass is still held in the church and every June a mayor is elected. Dating from the 12th century, many of the stone buildings have been abandoned. In winter the cobbled streets are empty, but in summer many people come here to eat and drink local specialities at **Humska konoba** (see ⑤). Call in for a glass of *biska*, a mistletoe drink unique to central Istria. Return to the main road and turn right. At Lupoglav, take the A8 motorway to Pazin to complete the circuit.

OPTIONAL SECOND DAY

If you have two days in central Istria, so much the better. For the first day follow the tour at a more leisurely pace as far as Grožnjan, then return to Motovun and stay overnight. The next day, carry in the direction of Buzet.

Istarske Toplice

Stop at the resort of **Istarske Toplice ⑦** (Sv. Stjepana 60; www.istarske-toplice. hr; daily 10am–8pm) for a swim in the thermal waters (in use since at least Roman times) or the luxurious indoor spa pool. Tucked under a 100m (330ft) high cliff, this scenic old health centre also offers the latest in wellness treatments.

Buzet

Next, follow the road east to **Buzet ⑧**. Look for the sign on the right to take you to Sovinjsko Polje and one of Istria's finest restaurants, **Toklarija** (see ⑥).

After lunch, continue to Buzet for a look around town and a stop at the **Regional**

Buzet, known as 'Truffle City'

Museum (Muzej; Mon–Fri 10am–3pm, summer also 5–8pm, Sat-Sun 10am–1pm, winter weekends by appointment; charge), which is housed in the 1639 Bigatto Palace. Don't forget to admire the ornate **municipal well** in the town centre.

Head on to Hum, but first make a stop at diminutive **Roč ❾** to look at the Romanesque **Church of Saint Anthony** (Crkva sv. Antuna) and Roman stone fragments.

Food and Drink

❶ MARINO

Gračišće 75, Pazin; tel: 052-687 081; www.konoba-marino-gracisce.hr; Thur–Tue 10am–10pm (11pm in winter); €€
At the entrance to nearly abandoned Gračišće is this restaurant-tavern. Vegetarians will have a tough time, but there's nothing industrial about the homemade sausages and home-smoked ham. You will need to book in advance.

❷ HOTEL KAŠTEL

Trg Andrea Antico 7, Motovun; 052-681 687; www.hotel-kastel-motovun.hr; daily 8am–10pm; €€
Shaded by trees, the terrace here has the best location in town. The restaurant, which serves dishes such as pasta with truffles and beef stew, is good but pricey; drinks are more reasonable. This is also a good option if you wish to stay a night in the region.

❸ KONOBA BASTIJA

Svibnja 1, Grožnjan; tel: 052-776 370; daily 11am–10pm; €€
Simple and casual, this local tavern serves up truffle-laced and hearty Istrian fare. Among its specialities are white truffles, game and wild mushrooms. Eat outside, on the terrace or indoors in an old-fashioned *konoba* with rustic tables and benches.

❹ ZIGANTE

Livade; tel: 052-664 302; www.restaurant zigante.com; daily 12–10pm; €€€
This is fine dining indeed. The chef here is devoted to showcase the truffle in all its glory. From starter to dessert, the taste of truffle perfumes each dish.

❺ HUMSKA KONOBA

Hum; tel: 052-660 005; www.hum.hr/ humskakonoba; mid-May–mid-Oct daily 11am–10pm, closed Mon mid-Mar–mid-May and mid-Oct–mid-Nov; weekends only mid-Nov–mid-Mar; €€
That humble Hum's name hasn't completely disappeared from the map is largely due to this restaurant. It's all about home cooking Istrian style with homemade *fuži* (pasta), long-simmering soups and fresh local ingredients.

❻ TOKLARIJA

Sovinjsko Polje 11; tel: 052-663 031; €€
In the heart of truffle country, it is no surprise that this prized delicacy features heavily. But you'll also find a wonderful asparagus salad and meat stewed on a wood-fired stove.

Split's harbour

SPLIT

Split offers a dynamic blend of pulsating nightlife, seaside strolls, ancient history and fascinating museums. Spend the morning exploring Diocletian's Palace and the Old Town, then walk along Marjan peninsula for great views.

DISTANCE: 11km (6.75 miles), including bus to Marjan peninsula
TIME: A full day
START: Diocletian's Palace
END: Veli Varoš
POINTS TO NOTE: This is a long day, so make an early start. If you prefer a more leisurely pace, you could devote the afternoon to either the museums or the walk across Marjan, instead of doing both. Most of Split's seaside promenade is closed to traffic; it is simplest to park in the car park between the Old Town and the bus, train and ferry arrival areas, and then proceed on foot.

Split is a busy, historic metropolis and a transport hub for central Dalmatia.

City beginnings

Split was founded by the Roman emperor Diocletian in AD295. Dalmatian by birth, he ordered the construction of a monumental palace in his homeland, then returned to spend the final years of his life here. With views over the Adriatic Sea and a backdrop of rugged mountains, the site he chose is magnificent.

During the 7th century, as hordes of Avars and Slavs rampaged through the region, inhabitants from the nearby Roman settlement of Salona took refuge within the palace walls, thereby marking the beginning of Split's development as a town. According to some sources, the name Split (Spalato in Italian) is derived from the Latin *palatium* (palace).

Layout

Split today is divided between the Old Town, within the walls of Diocletian's Palace, and a newer town that extends for 1km (0.75 mile) north, east and west of the palace. The further away from the Old Town, the more modern the architecture becomes, and not in a good way. Most of the city's restaurants, cafés and nightlife venues are to be found in and around the palace walls.

DIOCLETIAN'S PALACE

Begin the day with a coffee at any of the cafés along the seafront promenade (Riva

The Peristyle, Diocletian's Palace

or Obala Hrvatskog narodnog preporoda). The southern façade of **Diocletian's Palace** (Dioklecijanova palaca) provides a perfect suntrap, and the café terraces here remain open almost all year round.

The palace combined the qualities of a villa with those of a fortified military camp. Four sturdy outer walls each have a monumental gate that provides controlled access to the complex. This Unesco-listed palace resembles a walled medieval town with streets and passages surrounding a central square that is dominated by the cathedral. The southern façade, now giving on to the Riva, originally rose directly from the water, and boats could enter the complex from the sea.

Podrum

Walk along the Riva and find an opening between nos. 22 and 23 to enter the dark underground halls known as the **Podrum ❶**. This vast space served as a substructure to the palace above, and was probably used for storage. One passage through the halls leads to the Peristyle above and is lined with stalls selling pictures, ceramics, jewellery and handmade souvenirs.

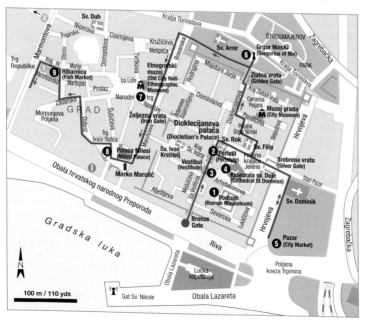

The cathedral's wooden doors, early 13th century

Peristyle
From the Podrum ascend a steep flight of stone steps to the **Peristyle ❷** (Peristil). In Diocletian's time this colonnaded square was the principal public space within the walls. Today, it remains a popular meeting point. During the summer festival, the Peristyle's dramatic quality sets the scene for outdoor opera and concerts.

Vestibule
Directly above the Podrum exit stands the **Vestibule ❸**, the grand entrance into Diocletian's seafront quarters. The domed roof would originally have been decorated with mosaics, and the walls faced with marble. Groups singing *klapa*, traditional Dalmatian plainsong (see page 20), are known to travel all the way from the islands to take advantage of the Vestibule's exceptional acoustics.

Cathedral of St Dominius
After Diocletian's death in AD316, his body was enclosed in a sarcophagus and placed in the centre of an octagonal mausoleum. Situated on the eastern side of the Peristyle, the emperor's resting place is now the **Cathedral of St Domnius ❹** (Katedrala sv. Duje; daily 8am–5pm, but the church can be inexplicably closed at times; charge), which is ironic because Diocletian despised Christianity and instigated the last great period of martyrdom for Christians. The fact that both his wife and daughter were Christians is something of an anomaly. Later inhabitants of the palace converted Diocletian's mausoleum into an early Christian church dedicated to St Domnius, after Bishop Domnius of Salona, who was one of the many victims of the purges.

As you enter the cathedral, note the original wooden doors, dating back to 1214. Carved by Andrija Buvina, a local sculptor, they depict 28 scenes from the *Life of Christ*. To the right of the cathedral bell tower sits a proud Egyptian sphinx from 1500BC, made of black granite.

You can climb the magnificent 13th-century **Romanesque bell tower**. From the top, some 60m (200ft) above the town, you can get a better perspective of the urban layout.

CITY MARKET

From the Peristyle, turn right on to Poljana kraljice Jelene to head for the city market. Leave the palace through the **Silver Gate** (Srebrena vrata), which was discovered and restored in the 1950s, having been concealed behind brick walls for centuries. The **City Market ❺** (Pazar; Mon–Sat 6am–1pm, Sun 6–11am) offers a chaotic array of seasonal fruit and vegetables, homemade cheeses and salamis, honey and herbal teas. If you are planning a picnic, this is where to pick up supplies.

Afterwards return to the Silver Gate and take the second turning on the right to pass through Poljana Grgura Ninskog. Turn left on Papaliceva, then right on Dioklecijanova, to reach the **Golden Gate** (Zlatna vrata), which was originally the main entrance into the palace.

The Vestibule's domed roof

The Iron Gate

GRGUR NINSKI

Just outside the gate stands an imposing statue of **Grgur Ninski ⑥** by Ivan Meštrović (1929), which was originally placed on the Peristyle to commemorate the 1,000th anniversary of the Split synod. Grgur was a 9th-century bishop who challenged Rome by advocating that the Croatian Church use the Slav tongue and Glagolitic script, as opposed to Latin. Tradition has it that if you touch the statue's toe and make a wish it will be granted.

NARODNI TRG

From the statue, follow the path right (west) through the garden that runs parallel with the outer walls, then turn left into Bosanska. You are now within the second area of town development. Follow Bosanska to **Narodni trg ⑦**, the main town square.

In the 11th century, Split enjoyed an era of material wealth and urban expansion. Medieval town houses sprouted alongside the wide thoroughfares of the ancient palace, resulting in a dark labyrinth of narrow walkways. Split also extended westward, and the **Iron Gate** (Željezna vrata) became the internal link between the old and new parts. When this newer zone was fortified in the 14th century, Narodni trg became the municipal centre, while the Peristyle remained the focus of religious activity.

Ethnographic Museum

The Venetians added a town hall on the square, identifiable by the Venetian-Gothic triple arches on the ground floor, which is now the **Ethnographic Museum** (Etnografski muzej; www.etnografski-muzej-split.hr; Sat 9am–1pm, also Oct–May Mon–Fri 9am–4pm, Sat 9am–1pm, June–Sept Mon–Sat 9.30am–8pm, Sun 9.30am–1pm; charge), displaying a collection of Dalmatian folk costumes. The complex originally included the adjoining Rector's Palace and a theatre that was demolished in 1821 by the Habsburgs. For their part, the Austrians erected a Secessionist building at the far end of the square.

TRG BRAĆE RADIĆA

Leave Narodni trg by Marka Marulića, a narrow street to your right as you face the Iron Gate and the 15th-century town clock. This will take you into **Trg braće Radića ⑧**, a small square one block back from the Riva, closed to the south by two octagonal 15th-century towers. At the square's centre stands a statue of **Marko Marulić** by Meštrović. The 15th century witnessed the birth of Croatian literature: Dalmatia was the centre of this movement, and Marulić's *Judita* (1521) is usually cited as the first play to be written in Croatian.

FISH MARKET

Walk the length of the square and take Dobrić, then turn left on Zadarska and immediately right on Obrov to arrive at the indoor **Fish Market ⑨** (Ribarnica; Mon–Sat 6am–noon, Sun 6–10am) on

At the Fish Market

Kraj sv. Marije. The peculiar smell here is not just the fish: next door stands another Secessionist building, which is the home of a private sulphur spa.

Lunch options

Now is a good time to consider lunch. If the fish market has inspired you, stop at nearby **Noštromo** (see ❶). Or for some of the best pizza in town, turn right on Marmontova, then take the second left for Tončićeva and **Galija** (see ❷). If you have picnic supplies, turn left on Marmontova, then right on the Riva, and stroll along the seafront to the gardens of the **Church of St Stephen** ❿ (Crkva sv. Stjepan) on the promontory, where you can eat in the shade of pine trees overlooking the sea.

ARCHAEOLOGICAL MUSEUM

After lunch you could visit the **Museum of Croatian Archaeological Monuments** ⓫

(Muzeja Hrvatskih arheoloških spomenika; Stjepana Gunjace; www.mhas-split.hr; Mon–Fri 9am–1pm and 5–8pm, Sat 9am–1pm; free) near St Stephen when you turn left on Šetalište Ivana Meštrovića. The museum traces the religious art of the first Croat settlers from the 7th to the 15th centuries. The exhibits are labelled in Croatian, but you can buy an English guidebook. Check out the outdoor terrace's group of *stećci*, monolithic tombstones dating back to the cult of the Bogomils (an anti-clerical, anti-imperial sect that enjoyed widespread popularity in the Balkans between the 10th and 15th centuries).

MEŠTROVIĆ GALLERY

A further 10 minutes along the same road you reach, at no. 46, the **Meštrović Gallery** ⓬ (Galerija Meštrović; www.mestrovic. hr; May–Sept Tue–Sun 9am–7pm, Oct–Apr Tue–Sat 9am–4pm, Sun 10am–3pm;

Sculpture, Meštrović Gallery

The peaceful Marjan peninsula

charge). Ivan Meštrović designed the villa as both a home and an exhibition space. Inside you can see his early pieces, heavily influenced by the Secessionist movement in Vienna where he studied. His later works on display here portray tortured, screaming figures that reflect the anguish he and millions of others suffered during World War II.

The gallery entrance ticket is also valid for **Kaštelet ⑬**, at no. 39, where you can see another Meštrović masterpiece: a series of woodcarvings portraying the *Life of Christ*, housed within a small church.

MARJAN PENINSULA

Round off the afternoon with a walk back to town across Marjan peninsula. Catch bus no. 12 from opposite Kaštelet, and disembark at the gateway into **Bene Beach ⑭**, which fringes the western edge of Marjan. The peninsula is planted with dense pine woods, and several well-kept paths offer beautiful views and a welcome retreat from city life.

Keep to the path along the southern side for the finest views, past the 15th-century **Church of St Jerome** (Crkva sv. Jere) and a medieval cave **hermitage** built into the cliffs. The walk, which takes about 40 minutes, ends at the 13th-century Romanesque **Church of St Nicholas** (Crkva sv. Nikola). Close by, the **Teraca Vidilica** terrace bar (see ③) is ideal for an apéritif.

Veli Varoš
Return to town via the stone steps of Senjska, passing through the appealingly ramshackle quarter of **Veli Varoš ⑮**. Continue down to Trumbićeva obala to try the hearty fare of **Fife** (see ④). Then continue east along the seafront back to the town centre.

Food and Drink

① NOŠTROMO
Kraj sv. Marije 10; tel: 091-405 6666; www. restoran-nostromo.hr; daily 6am–midnight; €€
So close to the fish market, Noštromo's seafood is as fresh as it gets – then simply but expertly prepared.

② GALIJA
Tončićeva 12; tel: 021-347 932; daily 11am–11pm; €
Pizzas here draw a faithful crowd. Salads and pastas round out the menu.

③ TERACA VIDILICA
Prilaz Vladimira Nazorov 1; tel: 095-871 8792; daily 8am–midnight
The setting here is stunning, with views of the sea, the islands, the harbour and city's terracotta rooftops.

④ FIFE
Trumbićeva obala 11; tel: 021-345 223; daily 6am–midnight; €
This casual place serves up simple but scrumptious plates of fried and grilled meat and fish, black risotto, and *palačinke* (pancakes) washed down by local wine.

The Roman ruins at Salona

AROUND SPLIT

This tour takes you along the coast to the evocative Roman ruins of Salona, on to the Unesco World Heritage Site of Trogir, then down to experience the Biokovo Nature Park, returning to Split with a stop at Baška Voda.

DISTANCE: 175km (109 miles)
TIME: A full day
START/END: Split
POINTS TO NOTE: A car is recommended for this route, but it can be done by public transport if you allow two days. From May to October there are regular shuttle boats from Split harbour to Trogir. Many bus services run down the coast serving Trogir, Solin, Makarska and Baška Voda from Split (see www.ak-split.hr). To visit the Biokovo Nature Park by 4x4, allow one day and leave Split early in the morning.

The suburbs of Split are unattractive and overdeveloped, but the sprawl eventually gives way to an indented coastline backed by high mountains. The towns and villages here are rich in history and architecture: a real break from busy Split.

GALONA

Leave Split and head north, following signs to Trogir. After a few kilometres you will reach Solin. Little more than a sub- urb of Split, Solin would be unremarkable except for the extraordinary Roman ruins of **Salona** ❶ on the suburb's outskirts. Park outside the main entrance, where there is a small **archaeological museum** (May–Oct Mon–Fri 7am–7pm, Sat 9am– 7pm, Sun 9am–1pm, Nov–Apr Mon–Fri 9am–3.30pm, Sat 9am–2pm; charge).

First on your left is **manastirine**, a vast necropolis where many of the Christian victims of Diocletian's persecution were buried. Follow the cypress-lined path south to Salona's city wall. South of the wall is a 1st-century covered **aqueduct**, and ahead are the remains of a 5th- century **cathedral** and **public baths**. But the highlight here is the **amphitheatre** at the western end, which could accommo- date up to 18,000 spectators.

TROGIR

After Solin turn off from the D8 and fol- low the old Adriatic highway (Jadran- ska magistrala) until it rejoins the D8 road further along the coast. After 20km (12.5 miles) you will arrive in **Trogir** ❷, a Renaissance jewel. Park in the large car

Trogir's charming Old Town

park on the mainland just north of the Old Town, which is situated on a small island between the mainland and Čiovo island.

To reach the Old Town, cross a small bridge at the southern end of the car park. Once on the island pause for a moment to admire the town walls. Protected by these thick walls and with the sea on one side and hills on the other, an extraordinary cultural life developed in Trogir from the 13th to 15th centuries. The finely adorned buildings in Trogir's medieval core recall the height of Dalmatian artistry, even as cafés, restaurants and souvenir shops crowd around them.

Cathedral of St Lawrence

Pass through the 17th-century Baroque **Land Gate** (Kopnena vrata) topped by a statue of the town's patron saint, St John of Trogir (Sv. Ivan Trogirski). Turn left then take the second street on the right to Trg Ivana Pavla II. Among the impressive buildings on this main square is the monumental **Cathedral of St Lawrence** (Katedrala sv. Lovrijenca; June–Sept 9am–noon and 4–7pm; charge), built between 1200 and 1598. The earliest and most beautiful feature is the main portal, richly decorated in Romanesque style, with saints, Apostles, animals and grotesques.

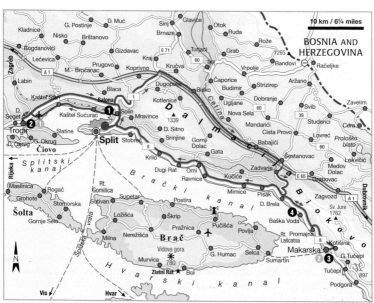

Kamerlengo Fortress

Trg Ivana Pavla II

Opposite the cathedral, the **Čipiko Palace** is a masterpiece by 15th-century sculptor Andrija Aleši showcasing fine Venetian-Gothic windows. The wooden figure of a rooster in the entrance was taken from the prow of a Turkish ship at the Battle of Lepanto in 1571.

The **15th-century loggia** across the square from the palace used to house the Hall of Justice. The stone table where the judges sat is still there, as is a relief depicting Justice and the two patron saints of Trogir on the wall behind. In contrast to these Renaissance works is the Modernist equestrian relief by Ivan Meštrović on the back wall.

Fish market

Leave the main square by Gradska ulica, to the right of the loggia. Follow this cobbled street to a second city gate, on the seaward side of town, dating from 1593. To the left the **16th-century loggia** now serves as a fish market. From here you have views across to the island of Čiovo, accessible by bridge. Proceed right along the seafront, past the white neo-Gothic school building, and on the right is **Fontana** (see ①), a great place for lunch.

Kamerlengo Fortress and Marmont's Pavilion

Further along the seafront is **Kamerlengo Fortress** (June–Sept 9am–8pm; charge), built by the Venetians in the 1400s as part of the city's fortification system. In summer it hosts an open-air cinema.

On the western tip of the peninsula stands a small neoclassical gazebo known as **Marmont's Pavilion**. Marshal Marmont, Napoleon's right-hand man during the time of the French occupation (1805–15), used to play cards and watch the sun set here on summer evenings.

MAKARSKA

Leave Trogir and return to Solin on the D8, then follow signs for the A1 motorway. Go southeast in the direction of Split and continue as far as Zadvarje, then follow signs south to the coastal road and **Makarska** ❸ (90km/56 miles from Trogir). Once in the centre admire the lovely Old Town built around a naturally protected bay, backed by the awesome Biokovo Mountain.

In the 15th century, while cities such as Split and Šibenik were protected by Venice from Turkish invasion, this stretch of coast fell to the Turks. The Ottoman conquerors made Makarska an important administrative centre and fortified the town with walls and three towers that sadly no longer exist.

Kačićev trg

Start on the seafront (Obala Kralja Tomislava), where **Hotel Biokovo** (see page 105) boasts a fantastic terrace bar. Head along the palm-lined promenade until you see an opening on the left leading to **Kačićev trg** and the 18th-century Baroque **Church of St Mark** (Crkva sv. Marko). The square also has some fine Baroque town houses, built by wealthy merchants in the 17th and 18th centuries.

Cathedral of St Lawrence   *Makarska sits below Biokovo Mountain*

Road to Kotišina

Behind the church is an open-air **food market** (open mornings only), with steps leading up to the busy main road. Cross the road and take Makra put, which leads you over another busy road, and continue until you see a turning to the right, Mlinica put. This brings you to the small village of **Mlinice** (Little Mills), where there is indeed a semi-preserved complex of watermills. Follow this road all the way up to a mountain path and a signpost to Kotišina. The 3km (2-mile) walk from Makarska to Kotišina takes about 50 minutes.

KOTIŠINA

Kotišina is a conglomeration of old stone houses built into a craggy hillside. Following an earthquake in 1962, the entire population moved down to Makarska. Villagers now keep their former homes as weekend retreats, returning to cultivate small vineyards and olive groves. Upon arrival, look out for a sign to the **Botanical Gardens** (Botanički vrt). More giant rockery than formal garden, it features a fine selection of indigenous plants and flowers.

Behind the garden, built into the cliff face, stands Kaštel. When the Turks conquered Makarska in 1499, the people of Kotišina defended themselves from this small fortress, which they had erected to blend perfectly with the surrounding rocks.

Return to Split

Return to Makarska's seaside promenade, with a choice of cafés, or head northeast to **Stari Mlin** (see ❷). Leaving Makarska, take the scenic D8 coastal road northwest and stop at the resort of **Baška Voda ❹**. It is easy to park along the sea for a quick swim or a snack on the waterfront before returning to Split via the D8 (42km/26 miles).

Brač

Half an hour from Split by ferry is **Brač**, Croatia's third-largest island and the location of **Zlatni Rat** (Golden Cape) near Bol. This shingle peninsula cuts scenically into the Adriatic, attracting countless sun-lovers and boat cruises during summer. Bol itself has a pleasant Old Town and is a centre for walks in the surrounding hills.

Food and Drink

❶ FONTANA

Obrov 1, Trogir; tel: 021-885 744; www.fontana-trogir.com; 9am–midnight; €€

Rare is the hotel restaurant that's worth a detour on its own merits, but Fontana is one of them. Grilled fish and seafood are the specialities, but there's also a choice of meat dishes as well as a mixed vegetable platter.

❷ STARI MLIN

Prvosvibanjska 43, Makarska; tel: 021-611 509; daily 11am–midnight; €€

A five-minute walk from the seafront, the fish specialities at this casual eatery are more affordable than on the waterfront.

KRKA NATIONAL PARK AND ŠIBENIK

Visit the splendid waterfalls, island monastery and traditional watermills of Krka National Park. Afterwards, stop at Šibenik to admire the Cathedral of St James, a World Heritage Site, and dine in an exquisite local restaurant.

DISTANCE: 158km (98 miles) round trip; Krka boat tour return trip: 32km (21 miles)
TIME: A full day
START/END: Split
POINTS TO NOTE: This route should be done by car, although it is possible by public transport. Take a bus to Šibenik from Split. At Šibenik hop on a bus to Skradin, one of the entrances to the National Park. Bring warm clothes if you travel upriver to Roški slap or Visovac, as it can get cool in the late afternoon. And bring your swimming gear.

The splendid network of lakes, cascades and rivers that make up **Krka National Park** (Nacionalni park Krka) are not only a natural wonder, but also form an important part of Croatia's cultural heritage. There's an Orthodox monastery far upriver, a Franciscan monastery and the region's first hydroelectric plant.

Leave Split early and take the A1 motorway north 74km (46 miles) to Skradin, located at the mouth of the River Krka.

KRKA NATIONAL PARK

Among the five entry points to the park, **Lozovac** in the south is the main one. There are smaller entry points at **Skradin** ❶, Roški slap, Burnum and Kistanje. This walk starts from the entrance at Skradin.

The waters of the River Krka are extraordinarily rich in fish, which explains the town's long history. Traces have been found of habitation here from the Palaeolithic era. It later became the Illyrian settlement of Scardona and then a Roman municipality. Its location put Skradin on a political fault line, and it passed many centuries seesawing between Croatian and Serbian rulers, and Venetian and Turkish occupiers. The 1990s conflict was more of the same for Skradin, which suffered consierable damage as the front line between the Croat-dominated municipality of Šibenik and the inland Serb-controlled area of Krajina. No traces of conflict are visible now on the quiet stone streets lined with prosperous shops and busy cafés.

Start at the **Krka National Park tourist office** (Obala Pavla Šubića; www.np-krka.hr; July–Aug 8am–9pm, Sept–June

Wooden path leading to Skradinski buk falls

9am–8pm) in the big glass building on the main road, not to be confused with the small Skradin tourist office (Trg Mate Gospe 3) on the harbour. The office will sell you an admission ticket and give you the schedule of boats running to Visovac and Roški slap. There are a number of grocery stores in Skradin to pick up picnic supplies.

Boats from Skradin to Skradinski Buk don't run from December (occasionally November depending on weather conditions) until March (again, weather permitting). The park is open all year round, but in winter it's best to use the entrance at Lozovac.

Skradinski buk

Take a national park boat (included in park entry fee) to **Skradinski buk** ❷ at the confluence of the green River Čikola and the blue River Krka. Here pay the fee at a small kiosk (if you have not already bought a ticket at the national park office in town), and take a narrow path that leads to a lovely grassy clearing surrounded by trees and overlooking the first series of waterfalls. It's a great place to picnic, and is also one of only two spots where swimming is allowed – in a roped-off area at a safe distance from the falls. Allow about 1.5 hours to explore Skradinski buk, more if you intend to swim.

Skradinski buk

Nearby, a wooden footbridge takes you across the river. The disused hydroelectric power station on the right was one of Europe's first; it dates back to 1895, when Šibenik was the first town in the Austro-Hungarian Empire to install electricity. Climb a flight of stone steps, make your way through the trees, past stalls selling walnuts, dried figs and bottles of *rakija*, and, once you have reached the top, you will have a stunning view of the waterfalls. A small **museum** in a renovated mill shows how local farmers used to bring their grain here to be milled while the women washed linen in the swirling waters.

Feast your eyes on the network of falls and streams, as the River Krka plunges down 17 cascades with a total drop of 46m (150ft) and a width of 200m (665ft). To experience the full panorama, follow the signs to **Lozovac**, the southern entrance to the park. The wooden walkways run through shady woods and over bubbling brooks for 1km (0.75 mile), and you will be treated to views of the falls from all angles.

Visovac

From Skradinski buk follow the signpost to the boat dock for the Visovac and Roški slap excursions. The trip upriver is magical as the blue waters meet the steep, rocky cliffs. From Skradinski buk there are only two or three boats a day (depending on the season) that go further upriver. One boat takes you on a 3.5-hour tour to Roški slap that includes a visit to Visovac. Another one or two boats make the two-hour trip to visit the Visovac monastery. There is an extra charge for these excursions, payable in Skradin or Skradinski buk.

Some 4km (2.5 miles) from Skradinski buk, **Visovac** ❸ is a tiny islet on which a perimeter of cypress trees shelters a 16th-century **Franciscan Monastery** (Franjevački samostan; www.visovac. hr). Even without the stunning setting, it would be worth coming here to see the first printed edition of *Aesop's Fables* (1487). Only two other copies of the book exist. Outside there is a lovely flowering garden, tended by the monks.

Roški slap

Boats stop at Visovac for about 20 minutes before continuing upstream to the park's most remote waterfalls, **Roški slap** ❹. The cliff walls seem to press in on you as the gorge narrows to a width of 150m (492ft). The 26m (84ft) high falls are bordered by watermills on one side, which you can visit, and at the top of the falls is a restaurant, **Roški slap** (see ❶), with panoramic views. The boat will take you back to Skradinski buk, from where you can catch the boat back to Skradin (on the half-hour).

Leave Krka by late afternoon, then take the local road to Šibenik, 9km (5.5 miles) southeast.

ŠIBENIK

The Old Town of **Šibenik** ❺, established by the Slavs in the 10th century, is built on a hill overlooking the Krka estuary. Steep, narrow, winding streets lead from the seafront to a hilltop fortress. Like Skradin, Šibe-

Cathedral of St James   *Outside the Cathedral*

nik bounced back and forth among rulers and occupiers, and was attacked by Yugoslav forces in 1991, dealing a serious blow to its economy. Many people are still out of work and tourism is negligible, as Šibenik is one of the few coastal towns without a beach. But it does have the finest cathedral in Dalmatia, perhaps in all Croatia.

Cathedral of St James

The Old Town is closed to traffic. From the car park at the eastern end of the seaside promenade walk along to the **Cathedral of St James** (Katedrala sv. Jakova; summer 8.30am–8pm, winter 8.30am–noon and 4–8pm; charge). Erected between 1431 and 1536, it displays a fine mix of late-Gothic and Renaissance architecture. Of the ornate Gothic portals, the main one, showing *The Last Judgement*, is surrounded by the Twelve Apostles and topped with a portrait of Christ; the side portal, depicting *Entrance to Paradise*, is guarded on either side by a lion, one carrying Adam, the other Eve.

The cathedral adopted Renaissance characteristics in 1441 when Juraj Dalmatinac, who was born in Dalmatia and trained in Venice, proposed the addition of a transept and apses to form a Latin cross, topped with a magnificent cupola. He also created an extraordinary frieze running around the outer walls that portrays 74 heads of diverse figures, wearing turbans, kerchiefs and ribbons. As Dalmatinac died before the building was finished, it was left to Nikola Fiorentinac to complete the roof and mount the splendid cupola.

Inside, to the right of the altar, the delightful Dalmatinac-designed baptistery was actually created by the sculptor Andrija Aleši. The stonework of this semi-underground cavern is carved as finely as lace, creating a marvellous sense of light and energy in a tiny space. As you leave, check out Ivan Meštrović's statue of Dalmatinac to the right of the main entrance.

If dinner beckons, **Gradska Vijećnica** (see ❷) is just across from the cathedral.

Back to Split

If time allows, take the coastal road to Split for the scenery, especially the view of **Primošten**, a tiny town crowded onto a peninsula. Otherwise, take the motorway for the 75km (46.5 miles) back to Split.

Food and Drink

❶ ROŠKI SLAP

Roški slap, Krka National Park; tel: 095-569 2176; www.roski-slap.com; daily lunch and dinner; €
Serves excellent local specialities, and there may well be freshly caught Krka fish too. However, the main attraction is the view.

❷ GRADSKA VIJEĆNICA

Trg Republike Hrvatske 3, Šibenik; tel: 022-213 605; Mon–Sat 9am–1am; €€€
This fine restaurant is set in a 16th-century Venetian loggia that is now the Town Hall. Sit outside to marvel at the cathedral while feasting on grilled scampi and fresh pasta.

Vis Town

VIS

This tour of idyllic Vis island takes in the fishing village of Komiža, Tito's Cave, the island's remote beaches and the historic town of Vis. Devote a second day to the unforgettable Blue Cave on Biševo island.

DISTANCE: 32km (20 miles)
TIME: One or two days
START/END: Vis Town
POINTS TO NOTE: You can reach Vis from Split by ferry or catamaran; but from June to September the schedule is more limited, making day trips difficult (for details see www.jadrolinija.hr). Note that to visit the Blue Cave, you must arrive the night before. For accommodation options see page 105. It's best to have wheels to visit Vis island, but consider renting a car, bike or scooter when you arrive. The price for bringing a car on to a ferry for a day trip can be more expensive than renting a car on arrival, and queues to get on the ferry can be long. Try Ionios (Obala sv. Jurja 37; tel: 021-711 532) or Navigator (Šetalište Stare Isse 1; tel: 021-717 786; www.navigator.hr). By public transport take the bus to Komiža that awaits the arrival of the morning ferry. Visit Komiža first and Vis Town when you take the afternoon bus back. Note that the Archaeological Museum of Vis Town is closed 1–5pm and on Sundays. Bring swimming gear.

Two and a half hours by boat from the mainland, mountainous Vis island is happy to get a stream of tourists in the summer and then equally happy to return to the main business of producing wine. The journey can be blissful on a fine day as the boat passes by Brač, Šolta and Hvar islands.

In World War II, the Yugoslav Partisans established their headquarters deep in the island's forested interior. Vis later became a military naval zone that was closed to foreigners until 1989. Thus, not only is the land forested and unspoilt, but the sea is teeming with fish. It is one of the most popular diving destinations in Croatia.

If you have your own wheels, you could visit Vis Town first. Otherwise, it is best to take the bus directly to Komiža. See www.info-vis.net for bus times.

KOMIŽA

From Vis Town take the road to **Komiža** ❶, which is a scenic 9km (5.5-mile) trip through the hilly interior. Your first view of Komiža is from the brow of the hill

above town, where a spectacular panorama opens up before you. The bus drops you almost in the centre of town, one block back from the Riva (seafront promenade) and the main square, **Škor**. The old stone buildings and narrow cobbled streets face south towards the harbour, and are protected to the north by a dramatic range of volcanic hills.

St Nicholas Monastery

Above the town the **Monastery and Church of St Nicholas** (Crkva sv. Nikola) are well worth visiting. These were founded in the 13th century by Benedictine monks, who had settled on nearby Biševo island two centuries earlier, but fled in fear of piracy. Every year on St Nicholas's Day (6 December),

locals gather in front of the church for a ceremonial burning of a fishing boat.

On the road up to the church of St Nicholas, note a track to the right and the *plaža* (beach) sign. The path runs down to the coast on the town's eastern side, where you will find rocky coves and secluded beaches, some of which are given over to nudism.

On the western side of town, just after Hotel Biševo, you will find another pebble beach and a bar. Nearby stands the 16th-century Renaissance **Church of Our Lady of the Pirates** (Crkva gospa gusarica), which, it was hoped, would protect the town from pirate attacks.

For lunch, try **Konoba Jastožera** (see ➊) in the centre of the harbour. After, if you have your own transport, it's time to explore the rest of Vis island. Otherwise, catch the bus back to Vis Town.

VINEYARDS

Once you have passed the Church of St Nicholas, the road weaves along high cliffs with majestic views of the sea to the right. The road takes you through the vineyards that produce Plavac, Vis's excellent wine, and some wineries are open to visitors. Around Podhumlje try **Cobo ➋** (tel: 021-713 750), and near Podšpilje

Tito's Cave

you will find **Vinarija Podšpilje** ❸ (tel: 021-715 054) among others.

TITO'S CAVE

Just before Podšpilje, a sign on the left directs you to Borovik, site of **Tito's Cave** ❹ (Titova špilja). It was in the midst of these forests that Tito and his Partisans took shelter from the Germans in a cave from June to October 1944 and co-ordinated military operations from there. A short hike up some steep steps takes you from the road up to the cave. There is not much to see, but it is a pleasant detour. Return to Borovik and take the country road to the village of **Žena Glava** ❺, with great views of the island and sea. You may wish to stop for refreshment at **Pol Murvu**, a local *konoba*, if it is open. From Žena Glava, you can return to the main road.

BEACHES

Return to the main road and turn left. After a few kilometres, you will see a sign on the right directing you to **Stiniva** ❻. The unpaved road takes you to the top of a cliff overlooking Stiniva Bay. It is a steep scramble to the bottom, but the unspoilt beach at the foot of this stunning bay is worth the trouble. Make sure you have enough water, as there are no facilities.

Back on the main road, continue east until a sign directs you to **Rukavac** ❼.

Here there is another idyllic beach, **Srebrna**, easily accessible via a path to the right of the small car park. The beach is rocky but lined with pine trees.

Take the main road heading north, and a few minutes later you will be back in Vis Town.

VIS TOWN

Vis Town ❽ (Grad Vis) was founded by the Greeks in the 4th century as Issa, and soon became a powerful city-state. Nevertheless, Issa lost its autonomy when the Romans took over in 47BC. In the Middle Ages there were two settlements – Luka to the west and Kut to the east – that today are joined to form a continuous urban complex stretching 3km (2 miles) around the bay. At the entrance to Vis harbour is an islet with a lighthouse named after Captain Hoste, head of the British fleet based here during the Napoleonic Wars. At the northern end of the harbour is the Prirovo peninsula, where George's Fortress, named after Britain's King George III, was built to protect Vis harbour.

Greek and Roman ruins

From the town centre and ferry dock, walk north along the seafront for about 100m/yds until the commercial area ends and you come to the tennis courts. Turn left and walk behind the tennis courts to find remains of the **ancient Greek cemetery**, which are right outside the walled town built by the Greeks.

The ancient Greek cemetery

You guessed it – the Blue Cave

You can still see remains of the **Greek walls**. Return to the seafront and continue walking north along the coast. After a few metres, across from the petrol station, you will see the remains of the **Roman baths**.

Archaeological Museum

Now walk in the other direction along the waterfront, passing the ferry dock. About 100m/yds later, on your right, is the **Archaeological Museum** (Arheološki muzej; June–Oct Mon–Fri 10am–1pm and 5–9pm, Sat 10am–1pm, out of season by appointment only; charge), which provides an excellent overview of Vis's fascinating history. The museum is lodged in an Austrian fort *(batarija)*, and contains one of Croatia's most extensive collections of Greek artefacts. The star of the collection is the bronze head of Aphrodite, sculpted in the 4th century BC.

For dinner, the most outstanding choice in town is the **Vila Kaliopa**, (see ②), located near the museum.

The Blue Cave

Biševo island, lying 5km (3 miles) southwest of Komiža, is home to the truly special **Blue Cave** (Modra špilja). Through a narrow sea corridor, you will find yourself floating in a blue chamber 24m (78ft) long and 12m (39ft) wide. The cave is magical at any time, but the best time is between 11am and noon when a strong shaft of sunlight bathes the interior in an unearthly blue glow.

A number of travel agencies in Komiža organise day trips to Biševo, also including bathing at Porat Bay, one of the few sandy beaches on the east Adriatic. Try Alternatura (Hrvatskih mucenika 2; tel: 021-717 239; www.alternatura.hr).

Lavender grows in the island's interior

HVAR

A tour of the island of Hvar, with its unspoilt coastline, fine wines and lavender fields. See fashionable Hvar Town, which features some of Dalmatia's most beautiful 16th-century buildings, then visit some of the island's most scenic towns and villages.

DISTANCE: Walking tour: 1.5km (1 mile); driving, returning via the hill villages: 67km (41.5 miles)
TIME: One or two days
START/END: Hvar Town
POINTS TO NOTE: This tour has two parts: a morning walk in Hvar Town and an afternoon driving tour of Hvar Island. With stops for sun and sea, either part can be stretched to a full day. Regular year-round ferries to Stari Grad on Hvar Island are run by Jadrolinija (www.jadrolinija. hr). Another option is to drive to Drvenik on the mainland and take a Jadrolinija ferry to Sučuraj then drive to Hvar Town. You could also take a passenger boat from Split directly to Hvar Town (www. krilo.hr). It's hard to get around Hvar by public transport, although there is a bus from Stari Grad to take ferry passengers to Hvar Town. You can also hire scooters or bikes. To avoid exploring in the heat of the day, try to be at the door when the first museum (the Arsenal) opens at 9am and finish when the last museum (the Franciscan Monastery) closes at noon.

Hvar Island is the sunniest spot in Croatia, receiving 2,724 hours of sunshine a year. Much of the island is lush and hilly, but there are fertile plains and an indented coastline. The eastern part of the island is much less developed and markedly more rural than the west.

HVAR TOWN

Entrancing **Hvar Town** ❶, with its elegant Renaissance churches and old stone buildings, is arranged around three sides of a picturesque harbour that is sheltered from the open sea by the scattered Pakleni islands, and backed by a hilltop fortress. Under Venetian rule (from 1331 to 1797), Hvar became one of Dalmatia's richest towns. Venetian merchant ships en route to the Orient would call here, and the town soon established its own fleet. Prosperity brought culture, which, coupled with a pleasant climate and plentiful local wine and fish, must have made for a good life.

Arsenal

Start at the harbour, which is packed with

Španjola citadel above town

flashy sailing boats in summer. At the northern end of the harbour is the **Arsenal**. Through a large arched entrance spanning 10m (33ft), workers pulled Venetian warships across the slipway and into the dry dock for repairs. The original 13th-century building was badly damaged during a Turkish invasion in 1571; the reconstruction of the present building was completed in 1612. It is currently undergoing extensive restoration.

The upper floor's **Arsenal Gallery** (Galerija Arsenal; Apr–Oct 9am–1pm and 5–11pm, Nov–Mar by appointment; charge) exhibits contemporary Croatian art, with an emphasis on Hvar artists. To the right of the entrance stands the *zvir* (beast), a wooden prow in the form of a dragon, taken from the Hvar city galleon following a famous victory over the Turkish navy at the Battle of Lepanto in 1571.

Theatre of Hvar

In the same building is the historic **Theatre of Hvar** (Hvarsko povijesno; closed for renovation). Opened in 1612, the theatre's tiny interior was redecorated in a neo-Renaissance style in the 19th century. This was the first theatre of its kind in Europe and, unusually, it welcomed all, regardless of social position. Theatre was not new to Hvar: in the 14th century miracle plays were performed in the square in front of the cathedral. These days, performances are restricted to special one-off events.

St Stephen's Square and Cathedral

Back outside you will find yourself on Hvar's main square, **Trg sv. Stjepana**, which was formed by filling in an inlet. At 4,500 sq m (about 48,500 sq ft), it is the largest piazza in Dalmatia, and certainly

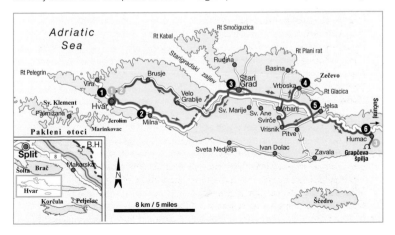

Café life in Hvar Town

one of the most beautiful. Walk its length to visit the Cathedral of St Stephen (Katedrala sv. Stjepana; daily 9am–noon and 5–7pm; free). The monumental Renaissance façade stands in harmony with the elegant 17th-century bell tower. A previous cathedral was destroyed by Turkish invaders in 1571, prompting the construction of this Venetian-style cathedral. The cathedral treasury is displayed in the **Bishop's Palace** (Riznica; summer 9am–noon and 5–7pm, winter 10am–noon; charge) just next door.

Only a few minutes' walk behind the cathedral is the **Summer Residence of Hanibal Lucić** (Ljetnikovac Hanibala Lucića; summer 9am–1pm and 5–11pm, winter 10am–noon; charge). Lucić (1485–1553) was a poet and playwright, and Hvar's most prominent citizen, whose romantic sensibility perfectly expressed his age. His Renaissance residence and gardens have been beautifully restored, displaying paintings and furnishings from the period.

Groda

North of the main square is Groda. Protected by the Španjola citadel, this was the aristocratic quarter, and still bears traces of the medieval palaces built after Hvar accepted Venetian rule in 1278. Grad is surrounded by 13th-century Romanesque walls, which are flanked by crenellated towers.

Take the street on the left as you face the cathedral, and take the first left on to Ulica Petra Hektorovića. Here you will

see the city's oldest well, dating back to 1475, bearing a figure of the Venetian Lion holding a closed book, symbolising that Venice was at war at the time.

At the end of the street, go up the stairs to the **Benedictine Convent** (Benediktinski samostan; summer daily 9–11am, 7–9pm; free), an austere building with paintings, objets d'art and elaborate silk embroidery and lacework woven by the nuns, dating from the 16th to 18th centuries.

Španjola citadel

Continue climbing the stairs and cross the road on top. Follow signs up to **Španjola**, the medieval citadel 90m (300ft) above sea level. Every Hvar ruling regime left its mark on the fortress, from the Venetians who strengthened it in 1557 to the Austro-Hungarians who added the barracks in the 1800s. Now it is a popular nightlife spot, **Veneranda**, with spectacular views. After a drink or an ice cream at one of the citadel cafés, if you have the energy you can continue the climb up to **Fort Napoleon** at 240m (786ft).

Gojava neighbourhood

Continue west along the harbour until you come to the **Nautika**, a popular bar at night. Turn right and you will come to the Church of St Mark, now a small **Archaeological Collection and Lapidarium** (Prirodoslovni kabinet Dr Grgur Bučic; summer 10am–1pm and 8–11pm, winter by appointment; charge). If you feel like a swim, continue on the same road

The Franciscan Monastery   *Moonlit Vrboska*

and after about 200m/yds you will come to the beach in front of the Hotel Amfora. Otherwise, return to the town centre and head south on Riva through the Burg neighbourhood.

Burg

In the 15th century, the plebeians of Hvar began building their houses south of the main square on the Glavica hill, now the location of many of the private rooms and apartments to rent. Continue following the harbour until you come first to a tiny pebble beach and then to the **Franciscan Monastery and Museum** (summer 10am–noon and 5–7pm, winter 10am–noon; charge). The Renaissance cloister is exquisite and often hosts classical music concerts in the summer. The 16th-century bell tower is equally stunning, built by stonemasons from Korčula. The monastery church contains several notable works of art. Note especially the polyptychs by the Venetian artist Francesco da Santacroce, and sculptor Leandro Bassano's *Crucifixion* on the altar. Below the altar is the tomb of Hanibal Lucić. The monastery's rectory houses a museum, which is also a repository for priceless art, especially *The Last Supper* by an unknown 17th-century Italian painter and an edition of Ptolemy's *Atlas* from 1524. Notice also the unusual clock designed to toll the work cycles of the monastery rather than the hours.

Lunch options

Walk back to town, where you can have lunch at **Bounty** (see ❶) on the other side of the port.

HVAR ISLAND

Milna

After lunch, head out of town towards Stari Grad. Take the 'new' road along the coast and make a stop at **Milna** ❷. This village sports two gravel beaches separated by a pine cove in a protected harbour, and offers a quiet respite from busy Hvar. Return to the road and continue on to Stari Grad.

Stari Grad

Now Hvar Island's principal ferry port, **Stari Grad** ❸ is the oldest settled part of the island. Colonised by the Greeks in the 4th century BC, this rather workaday town bears few remnants of its illustrious heritage, although it is pleasant enough to stroll around the harbour. The most interesting sites are the Dominican Monastery (summer daily 10am–noon, 6–8pm; charge) and Tvrdalj (summer daily 10am–noon and 6–8pm; charge), a castle that once belonged to Petar Hektorović, a renowned 16th-century poet whose most famous poem, 'Fishing and Fishermen's Conversations', is honoured by a fish pond within the walls.

Vrboska

Watch for the sign on the left on the road out of Stari Grad taking you to **Vrboska** ❹, Hvar's smallest town. At the end of a

Church of St Mary, Vrboska

bay lined with pine forests, a narrow canal bisects the town, which is often called 'Little Venice'. Vrboska was founded in the 15th century, and a surprising number of houses remain from the 16th to 19th centuries. Immediately on entering the town you will notice the picturesque stone bridges lined by typical Dalmatian village houses to your right.

Cross the bridge ahead of you and walk to your left along the harbour. After about 50m/yds take the narrow alley on your right to come to the unusual **Church of St Mary** (Crkva sv. Marija; open for Mass only). Fearing attacks by the Turks, the villagers rebuilt the existing 15th-century church into a real fortress, which is unique in Dalmatia. From the top, there are sweeping views. Paintings from the Church of St Mary are currently on display in the nearby **Church of St Lawrence** (Crkva sv. Lovre; summer 10am–noon and 5–7pm).

Return to the main road, turn left and continue on to Jelsa, Hvar island's other resort town. The journey takes you past a purple haze of perfumed lavender fields. Various herbs – lavender, rosemary, sage, marjoram and thyme – have been cultivated here since ancient times.

Jelsa

Although it may not have the glitz and glamour of Hvar Town, the small fishing town of **Jelsa** ❺ makes a good second choice for an island base. The buildings by the harbour date from the 19th century, when the shipping industry flourished. Call at **Villa Verde**, an appealing cocktail bar, for a drink on the Riva. From here visit the exquisite miniature Baroque **Church of St Ivan** (Crkva sv. Ivana; usually open in the morning, but times are irregular), one block back from the harbour. After a stroll around the **Old Town** at the foot of the harbour, you may wish to take the coastal promenade that runs from the southwest corner of the harbour and curves around the bay 400m/yds to the sandy **Mina cove**, a good place for a swim.

Humac

From Jelsa, return to the main road, and follow it the direction of Sućuraj (on the eastern tip of the island). **Humac** ❻ lies 6.5km (4 miles) east of Jelsa. Look out for a wooden hand-painted sign on the right, then park the car off the road and walk the final 400m/yds along a track to arrive at this romantic cluster of semi-abandoned, traditional stone houses.

Humac was founded in the 13th century as a shepherds' settlement. In later years, many inhabitants moved to the more sheltered and better-connected village of Vrisnik. For some years they returned to Humac to work the land, trekking three hours each way by mule or donkey. Today families from Vrisnik still cultivate these fields – keeping goats and growing vines, olives and lavender – more for pleasure than profit. Follow the old donkey path up the hill behind Humac to arrive at the summit, which has great views of the south-fac-

Breakfast in Jelsa   *Sveti Klement, one of the Pakleni islands*

ing slopes, the small island of Šćedro below and Korčula in the distance.

About 20 minutes from here on foot and signposted from the village is Grapčeva Cave (Grapčeva špilja; free), a vast underground chamber of stalactites, stalagmites, halls and chambers.

Before leaving Humac, have dinner at the unique and unforgettable **Konoba Humac** (see ❷). Then return to Hvar Town by the same route; or, if you have time, you may wish to explore some of the island's hill villages.

The Pakleni islands

You can see the Pakleni islands glittering just offshore in the midday sun, scattered like jewels on the Adriatic. Although the literal translation is 'Hell's Islands', in fact the name is probably derived from the word *paklina*, which is a special resin that was once used to coat ships. The island closest to Hvar is Jerolim, a favourite of naturists, although there are also 'clothed' beaches. Nearby is Marinkovac island with Stipanska Beach. The largest island is Sveti Klement, famous for the gorgeous Palmižana hamlet. Here, gentle waves lap at a sandy cove ringed by pine trees. It is the Adriatic at its best. From Hvar Town, regular excursion boats make the run to one or more of the islands.

Hvar's hill villages

From Humac, take the country road from Jelsa to Pitve, which was settled by the ancient Illyrians. From here, it is an easy drive to Vrisnik, another peaceful inland village. Return to the main road and head to Stari Grad. This time, take the country road that winds through the hills. Look for the sign on the left pointing you to Grablje and travel about 2km (1.25 miles) on an unpaved road to arrive at this nearly abandoned town with splendid views of the surrounding hills. Return to the main road and keep going until Brusje, an appealing clutter of stone houses only 5km (3 miles) northeast of Hvar Town.

Food and Drink

❶ BOUNTY

Fabrica bb; tel: 021-742 565; daily 10am–10pm; €€
In expensive Hvar, Bounty's fixed-price lunch menu is a relative bargain. The grilled fish, meat and pasta are correctly – if simply – prepared. Located on the western side of the harbour.

❷ KONOBA HUMAC

Humac; tel: 091-523 9463; summer Mon–Sat lunch and dinner; €€
Homemade food and drink from home-grown, home-brewed, home-caught or home-raised ingredients – you really can't get more traditional than this. There is no electricity here; the food is cooked on the barbecue or under a *peka* (which will need to be ordered in advance). Call before as opening times can be somewhat unpredictable.

DUBROVNIK

This day in the beautiful city of Dubrovnik takes in an exploration of the main thoroughfare and city walls, followed by a visit to the city's museums. Afterwards, tour the cathedral and enjoy sunset drinks.

DISTANCE: 3km (2 miles), including tour of city walls
TIME: A full day
START: Pile Gate
END: Synagogue
POINTS TO NOTE: Make an early start, as the walk around the city walls offers little shade: from noon onwards in summer it is extremely hot. It can also get uncomfortably crowded when cruise ships dock and several thousand people can descend on the city each day in high season. This route is intended as an introduction to the city; Dubrovnik has so much to see that to do it justice you really need more than one day. If you have more time, check out our *Insight Explore Guide: Dubrovnik*, which has 11 easy-to-follow routes around the city. Dubrovnik is well connected by bus to other Croatian cities and by a twice-weekly ferry to the island of Korčula (www.jadrolinija. hr). There's also an airport south of town, but there are no trains to Dubrovnik. If you arrive by car, note that the Old Town is pedestrian only, but there is parking on the north, east and west entrances to the town.

Dubrovnik, the Pearl of the Adriatic, lies on the southeastern tip of Croatia. Dubrovnik's walled Old Town is small, with a circumference of a little more than 1.5km (1 mile). To the east of the Old Town is the Ploče neighbourhood, with several luxury hotels and residences; to the southwest is the neighbourhood of Lapad, where most beaches and hotels are located; and to the northwest is Gruž, the harbour from where ferries run up the Dalmatian coast, as well as to the nearby Elaphiti islands, Mljet and Korčula.

STRADUN

Begin from the main entrance into town, **Pile Gate ❶** (Pile vrata), approached over a wooden drawbridge on chains. The gate was constructed in 1537, with a Renaissance arch topped by a statue of St Blaise (Sv. Vlaho), protector of the city, displayed in a richly decorated niche. The inner gate displays a sculpture of St Blaise by Ivan Meštrović. Once within the walls, you will notice a set of steep steps imme-

Dubrovnik's picturesque harbour

diately to the left, giving access to the ramparts.

But first stroll along **Stradun** (also called Placa), the Old City's main thoroughfare, which was created when the channel that once separated Dubrovnik from the mainland was filled in. In the evening, this is where local people stroll before taking a seat at one of the pavement cafés, while their children eat ice creams and play.

The Baroque buildings along Stradun are astonishingly uniform, each being of equal height and similar proportions, with green-shuttered windows and space for shops on the ground floor. They were erected according to strict regulations following the 1667 earthquake; the harmonious arrangement of these buildings is a large part of Dubrovnik's architectural appeal.

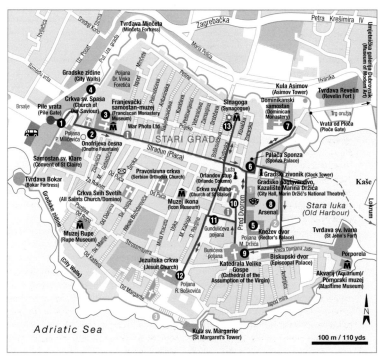

Pile Gate

Franciscan Monastery

At the Pile Gate end of Placa, the most striking monument is the circular **Onofrio Fountain ❷** (Onofrijeva česna), which still spouts fresh water. Built in 1438, the fountain is adorned with 16 carved masks. The water comes from a well 12km (7 miles) away, and supplied residents with drinking water during the bombardment in 1991.

To the left is the entrance to the **Franciscan Monastery ❸** (Franjevački samostan; Apr–Oct 9am–6pm, Nov–Mar 9am–5pm; charge), a sober structure with a remarkable carving of the **Pietà** over the entrance that dates from 1498. The interior is known for its **cloister**, constructed in the mid-14th century. The capitals of each double column are topped with figures of people, animals and flowers, and the interior garden is fragrant with herbs and fruit trees. Also in the monastery is a **pharmacy** that has been dispensing natural and other concoctions since 1391; it is the third-oldest pharmacy in Europe. You might also take a look at the monastery museum, which displays a mix of pharmaceutical equipment, relics, gold work, medical books and paintings.

Church of Our Saviour

Beside the monastery is the Renaissance **Church of Our Saviour** (Crkva sv. Spasa), built in 1520, in gratitude for the city's survival after a potentially destructive earthquake. Strangely, it was one of the few structures to withstand the earthquake of 1667. The acoustics of the church have made it a favourite concert venue.

Historical overview

After the Slavs ravaged the Roman city of Epidaurum (Cavtat) in the 7th century, the survivors took refuge on an island, which they named Ragusa. The settlers built walls and the Republic of Ragusa was established in 1358, when Hungary granted the city freedom. By the 1500s, Ragusa had a highly respected merchant navy, and shipbuilding developed apace. In 1667, however, the city-state suffered a devastating earthquake which destroyed its Renaissance architecture. The republic rebuilt; by the end of the 18th century and despite an economic recession, Ragusa had 673 ships and consulates in 80 cities. Yet after 450 years of liberty, the Ragusa Republic fell to Napoleon in 1808, and after the French were expelled in 1813, it became part of the Austro-Hungarian Empire until World War I. With the establishment of the Kingdom of Yugoslavia in 1929, the name Ragusa was dropped because it was deemed too Italian, and Dubrovnik took its place.

CITY WALLS

The tour of the **City Walls ❹** (Gradske zidine; Apr–Sept daily 8am–6.30pm or

Stradun *Touring the city walls*

7.30pm, till 5.30pm in Oct, Nov–Mar 9am–3pm; charge) can be commenced from the Pile Gate, from the equally imposing **Ploče Gate** (Vrata od Ploča) to the east, or from a third entrance by **St John's Fort** (Tvrđava sv. Ivana). The tour will take at least an hour to complete, the circuit being about 1.5km (1 mile) long, with lots to see en route. During high season, it will take considerably longer, as the footpaths will be crowded.

The fortification system dates back to the 13th century, although, as fear of foreign attack grew, the walls were further reinforced with additional towers and bastions. Cannons were positioned along the ramparts, and a deep trench was dug on the inland side.

The views over the sea are idyllic, as are vistas over the city from any part of the walls. All the damage to the terracotta rooftops inflicted during the 1991–2 bombardment has been carefully repaired. The glossy new roof tiles are the only sign of the widespread damage and renovation.

When you have completed a circuit of the walls, return to Stradun and make your way to Luža for Dubrovnik's imposing **Clock Tower** (Gradski zivonik), which first tolled the hours in 1444. On your right is the **Orlando Column** (Orlandov stup), sculpted in 1417 to honour the legendary Frankish knight Roland. His forearm was the official measure of the Ragusan Republic. On your right you will see the café/wine bar **La Bodega** (see ❶), a great place to take a break.

RECTOR'S PALACE

Next to Gradska Kavana is the **Rector's Palace** ❺ (Knežev dvor; closed for renovations). The rector was a civic leader (with no ecclesiastical connection) chosen from the city's nobility. To avoid the concentration of power in one individual, a new rector was elected every month. He was obliged to reside here, and could leave only for official business.

The Rector's Palace was plagued by disaster: the original building was destroyed by a gunpowder explosion, the next one by fire, and the third by the 1667 earthquake. The present building, dating from 1739, is largely Baroque, although some Gothic details have survived, and there are some wonderful carvings on the capitals of the columns. At ground level, looking onto the courtyard, were official state offices, a meeting room and the jail (now part of the museum). At the far end of the courtyard stands a bust of **Miho Pracat**, a wealthy merchant who bequeathed one ton of gold to Dubrovnik, and to the left, below the stairs, a Gothic well.

SPONZA PALACE

On leaving the Rector's Palace, cross over Stradun to the **Sponza Palace** ❻ (Palača Sponza; daily 10am–10pm, but opening hours can be sporadic; free). This is one of the few buildings that survived the 1667 earthquake,

The Dominican Monastery cloister

giving us some idea of what Dubrovnik architecture looked like before the quake. Built in the early 16th century, it displays a combination of Renaissance and Gothic styles, typical of palaces built on the eastern Adriatic coast before the arrival of the Baroque tradition. In the time of the republic, the Customs Office was located here, hence the word *Dogana* ('Customs' in Italian) on the metal-studded door. One room in the palace has become the **Memorial of the Defenders of Dubrovnik**, a moving dedication to those who died during the 1991–2 bombardment.

DOMINICAN MONASTERY

From the palace, take the narrow passage into the city walls. On the left is the **Dominican Monastery and Museum** ❼ (Muzej Dominikanskog samostana; daily 9am–6pm; charge), which contains Dubrovnik's most valuable paintings. The Dominican monks took no chances with their treasure when, in the 14th century, they built their monastery to look like a fort. The interior is much more elegant, however, with a cloister that rivals that of the Franciscan Monastery. Cavtat artist Vlaho Bukovac (1855–1922) contributed a wonderful pastel of *St Dominic* in the monastery church, and Titian's *Mary Magdalene* (*c*.1550) in the sacristy is a must-see. Unsurprisingly, the church was a prestigious final resting place

for Dubrovnik's noblest families. The monks also took it on themselves to support local artists, and the museum exhibits the apotheosis of the 15th- and 16th-century Dubrovnik school, with works by Nikola Božidarević, Lovro Dobričević and Mihajlo Hamzić. The triptych by Božidarević, showing Dubrovnik in the hands of St Blaise, is particularly interesting.

OLD PORT

Head to the Old Port on the east side of the town walls just behind the Rector's Palace. In the morning, small excursion boats to Cavtat, Lokrum and the Elaphiti islands leave from here. The Old Port is dominated by the arched entryways of the **Arsenal** ❽, where the republic's battleships were built and docked. From here you can see the **Lazareti**, on the coast to the left. This is where, in an effort to prevent the spread of infectious diseases, foreign sailors, travellers and merchants were held in quarantine. Today it is the city's premier arts venue, with cinema nights, folklore performances, club nights and artists' workshops.

DUBROVNIK CATHEDRAL

From the southern end of the Old Port turn right on Kneza Damjana Jude to reach the **Cathedral** ❾ (Katedrala; usually open 8am–8pm; free, small charge for treasury), a splendid

The impressive bulk of the Jesuit Church

example of 17th-century Baroque. A 12th-century Romanesque cathedral on the same site was partially funded (it is said) by England's King Richard the Lionheart, as a token of gratitude for having survived a shipwreck near the island of Lokrum on his return from the Crusades in 1192. During restoration work in 1981, foundations of an even earlier church, dating from the 7th century, were discovered. The severe modern altar and arrangement of three seats for the clergy were designed to mirror the plan of the ancient church.

Treasury

The **Treasury** (Riznica) has a horde of richly decorated gold and silver reliquaries. Among the most precious pieces is the head of St Blaise encased in a gold Byzantine imperial crown embellished with precious stones. The saint's arm and leg are also on display. Most of these objects originate from the East, and arrived here courtesy of the Dubrovnik naval fleet.

CHURCH OF ST BLAISE

Follow the street in front of the cathedral until you reach the 18th-century **Church of St Blaise** ❿ (Crkva sv. Vlaho; irregular opening hours; free). Named after the patron saint of Dubrovnik, the church overlooks Stradun and is the frequent focal point of public events and celebrations. Built

to replace an earlier church destroyed in the 1667 earthquake, St Blaise's ornate exterior is a fine example of Baroque style. Above the marble altar stands a silver figure of St Blaise that is paraded through the streets on 3 February each year during one of the biggest festivals of the winter. The saint is portrayed holding a scale model of the city, providing one of the few records of what the city-state looked like before the 1667 earthquake.

Behind the Church of St Blaise is the pretty **Gundulićeva poljana** ⓫ (Gundulić Square), surrounded by old stone houses and dominated by a monument to Ivan Gundulić, the city's greatest poet. A colourful fruit and vegetable market is held here each morning; when it ends, the stalls are replaced by tables set up by a number of restaurants, and becomes a relaxing, casual spot in which to dine. Continue through the square and take the steps at the far end to the Jesuit Church.

JESUIT CHURCH

From the square, turn left and take the broad flights of steps up to the **Jesuit Church** ⓬ (Jezuitska crkva; daily 8am–6pm; free). Also called the Church of St Ignatius (Crkva sv. Ignacija), it is one of Dalmatia's finest examples of early 18th-century Baroque architecture, designed by the Jesuit architect Ignazio Pozzo, who modelled the interior on the Gesù Church in Rome. Next

Buža Bar's spectacular setting

Elaphiti islands day trip

The Elaphiti archipelago northwest of Dubrovnik comprises 13 islands of which only three are inhabited: Koločep, Lopud and Šipan. The island closest to Dubrovnik is the diminutive and densely forested Koločep, whose two little settlements have a combined population of fewer than 200 people.

Lopud is slightly larger with a population between 200 and 300, but it was once a major port. In the 15th and 16th centuries, Lopud had a fleet of some 80 vessels and a shipyard. Many wealthy men built summer villas here, but little remains. From the harbour turn left at the stone well and you will come to the dilapidated Knežev dvor (Rector's Palace); look out for the splendid 15th-century Gothic windows. Return to the harbour and, beside an imposing church, you will see a sign for the now abandoned Grand Hotel. Take the path marked Plaža Sunj beside the Grand Hotel and follow it for about half an hour through fields of aromatic herbs until you come to one of the region's rare sandy beaches.

It's possible to visit Koločep and Lopud independently by taking a morning ferry to Koločep, visiting for an hour or so and then taking the next ferry to Lopud. Otherwise, take one of the organised tours that visit Koločep, Lopud and Šipan islands. See www.jadrolinija.hr for the ferry schedule and www.atlas-croatia.com for tour information. Boats leave from Gruž harbour.

to the church is the Jesuit College, where many of the city's notables were educated.

PRIKEKO

Now return to Stradun, cross over and take any of the 14 narrow uphill streets that run to the northern section of the city walls. These pretty stairways are cut by Prijeko, a long, straight street whose numerous restaurants and bars are located in the most popular – but not the best – quarter for eating out. The tall, narrow dwellings in these streets are humbler than the palaces found on the other side of town. Try to duck into the **Synagogue** ⑬ (Sinagoga; Žudioska 5; Sun–Fri 10am–8pm; charge), which is the oldest Sephardic synagogue in Europe. It also contains an intriguing little museum with ancient Torah scrolls and information about Dubrovnik's historic Jewish community.

SUNSET DRINK

An excellent way to finish the day is with a sunset drink at **Buža Bar** (see ❷). Head to the southern walls and follow Od Margarite until you see the sign saying 'Cold drinks with the most beautiful view'. Go through the hole in the wall and you will come to a bar with tables and chairs spread out on the rocks. If you are staying for dinner, try **Dundo Maroje** (see ❸).

Cavtat's rooftops and mountainous interior

MORE SIGHTS

With more time to spend, you could walk from the Ploče Gate, past Banje Beach and the Lazareti to visit the **Museum of Modern Art** (Umjetnička galerija Dubrovnik; Put Frana Supila 23; www.ugdubrovnik.hr; Tue–Sun 9am–8pm; charge). Alternatively, take a boat from the Old Port to the island of **Lokrum**, for a swim and a picnic under the pine trees. As with parts of Dubrovnik itself, Lokrum became one of the locations for the HBO fantasy drama series *Game of Thrones*. A slightly longer trip will take you down the coast to the lovely little port of **Cavtat**. All the boat trips are widely advertised on the quayside. For a vivid illustration of the horrors of the 1990s war, see the **War Photos Limited gallery** (Antuninska 6; www.warphotoltd.com; June–Sept daily 10am–10pm, May, Oct Wed–Mon 10am–4pm, closed Nov–Apr; charge).

Dubrovnik beaches

Dubrovnik is more than a treasured Old Town; it is also a place to relax by the beach and enjoy the pine-scented air. Dubrovnik's most popular beach is the sandy Copacabana Beach on the Babin Kuk peninsula. The shallow water makes it the best beach for children. Nearest to town is the gravel Banje Beach, near the chic Banje Beach Restaurant and Club (formerly the EastWest Club). Further along is the sheltered Sveti Jakov beach. Much accommodation is on the Lapad peninsula, which also has a string of pebble beaches.

Food and Drink

① LA BODEGA
Lučarica 1; tel: 095-234 4234; daily 8am–2am; €
You get some great people-watching on the wide terrace along with large platters of cured meats and cheeses in this lively wine bar right by the Church of St Blaise.

② BUŽA BAR
Od Margarite; summer daily 9pm–2am; out of season on sunny days; €

There's no better place to watch the sun set and contemplate the wonders of Dubrovnik than from this cocktail bar on the rocks. No food served.

③ DUNDO MAROJE
Kovačka bb; tel: 020-321 021; daily 11am–midnight; €€
Tucked away on a little side street, this restaurant has never lost its local appeal despite the waves of visitors crowding the outdoor tables. The fish and seafood dishes are prepared Dubrovnik style and the black risotto (*crni rižot*) is among the best in town.

MLJET

Spend a day or two in lush Mljet island and enjoy its beaches, forests and dazzling scenery. Visit the two inland lakes and island monastery of the wooded National Park; walk and cycle along shady trails, and swim or kayak on the crystal-clear lakes.

DISTANCE: Round trip, including boat tour: 9.5km (6 miles)
TIME: One or two days
START/END: Polače
POINTS TO NOTE: The G&V line catamaran Nona Ana (www.gv-line.hr) leaves Dubrovnik's Gruž harbour, at 9am every day June–September, with more sporadic crossings in winter excluding January–March. Tickets go on sale at the dock one hour before departure and cannot be booked in advance. It's also only for foot passengers. Alight at the second port of call, Polače, about 1.75 hours' journey away, not at the first stop, Sobra (unless catching the car ferry, see page 129). If you are staying overnight, contact the tourist board (www.mljet.hr) in advance to arrange accommodation in pretty Babine Kuće or, failing this, in Pomena. Take a torch, as paths have no lights.

Mljet is an island of steep rocky slopes, dense pine forests and dramatic views. It is one of the few Dalmatian islands that was never ruled by Venice, which is why no great towns were founded here. Indeed, Mljet has survived the centuries in a state of relative isolation. What it has lost in terms of grand architecture, however, has been more than compensated by the preservation of indigenous forests. More than 72 percent of the island is covered with Aleppo pines, umbrella pines, holm oak and maquis, making Mljet the most thickly wooded island in the Adriatic. Tourism is kept to a minimum; the inhabitants are committed to tending their olive trees, vineyards and fruit orchards.

Mljet National Park (Nacionalni park Mljet) on the island's western end protects 31 sq km (12 sq miles) of woodland and two inland seawater lakes. Legend has it that Odysseus stopped here on his voyage and stayed for seven years.

VELIKO JEZERO

Buy your park entrance tickets at the kiosk in the port of **Polače** ❶ (if you are staying overnight the charge may be covered in the cost of your accommodation), and a bus will take you on a five-minute ride to

A third of Mljet is protected as a national park

Pristanište on the shore of **Veliko Jezero** (Big Lake). It is actually a tidal expanse of salt water that lies with the national park.

For a leisurely look at Veliko jezero, take the path that runs along the lake 2km (1.25 miles) east to **Soline**, which is little more than a scenic scattering of houses on the lake.

A shorter path runs 500m/yds west to **Babine Kuće**, a small cluster of old stone houses with flowery gardens, overlooking the lake. Both places have private accommodation, but many devoted visitors return on an annual basis, so rooms can be difficult to find.

St Mary's Island

Return to Pristanište, where you can board a small boat (10 minutes past each hour; fare included in entrance price) that will take you out to the **St Mary's Island ❷** (Otok sv. Marija) in the middle of the lake. The church and remaining parts of the monastery on the island are Romanesque and date from the 12th century, but there were a number of 14th-century additions. Further changes were made in the subsequent 200 years when it gained a Renaissance façade. After the monks abandoned the place in 1808, it fell into disrepair, and is now being renovated by the St Mary's Foundation, in conjunction with the Diocese of Dubrovnik.

The church, an imposing single-naved structure, can be visited, but the monastery and cloister are still under wraps and closed to the public. However, the ground floor functions as the **Restaurant Mel-**

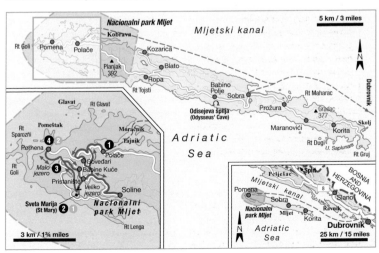

Pine groves provide much needed shade

ita (see ❶). It's a pleasant place to have an early lunch, although the setting can often be better than the food.

Before you eat, however, you might like to wander along the shady island paths. This stroll won't take more than 15 minutes, even if you stop to visit the two little votive chapels built by grateful sailors who had survived watery misfortunes. Alternatively, follow the coastal path for about 200m/yds from the monastery to find a good swimming spot from the rocky shore. If it is too early for lunch, treat yourself to a cool drink and an ice cream on the restaurant terrace, before getting the boat back to shore (45 minutes past each hour).

MALO JEZERO

The trip will not go directly to your starting point, but will take you to **Mali Most** (Small Bridge) on the edge of **Malo Jezero** ❸ (Small Lake), the second of the national park's lakes. Here, there's a small swimming beach and kayaks, canoes and rowing boats for hire. The water here is warmer than in the sea, so swimming is pleasant even in spring and autumn. Water enters the lakes through a narrow channel from the sea: if you stand at Mali Most you can see the water change direction with the tides.

A path marked 'Pomena' takes you round the side of Malo Jezero on a pleasant walk bordered by pines and olive trees, and with bright yellow butterflies swooping along ahead of you.

POMENA

After a while the path leaves the lake and goes up a fairly gentle wooded hill, then descends to the little settlement of **Pomena** ❹. Once a tiny fishing village, it is now Mljet's tourist centre, albeit a restrained and pretty one. The **Hotel Odisej** (see page 109), the only official hotel on the island, dominates the bay. Some smart yachts bob in the water, and there are several modest restaurants, as well as the one attached to the hotel.

Follow a path round to the right of the harbour to find a row of little eating places. **Barbe Ive** (see ❷) is right on the waterfront and specialises in seafood. There are more opportunities to rent bikes in the village. You could also rent one of the dune buggies available, which is a fun and more unusual way of exploring the island.

POLAČE

To get back to Polače, return to Pristanište and follow the sign. Rather than taking the paved road that veers to left, bear right and take the pedestrian path, Stari Put, back to town. Back in Polače, you could wander around the ruined walls of a Roman palace (the Romans founded Polače in the 1st century BC), but this won't detain you for long. Better to sit in one of the cafés that line the waterfront, enjoy the smell of wood smoke as restaurateurs fire up their barbecues, and try the local dessert wine, *prošek*, while you wait for the catamaran.

Polače harbour restaurant

St Mary's Island

EASTERN MLJET

Beyond the national park is a whole idyllic island waiting to be discovered. You will need to have a car or some form of private transport to do it justice, though. Take your car on to the ferry to **Sobra** (or rent a car from the Mini Brum agency at the Sobra port; tel: 020-745 084). From Sobra take the main road heading east. The route is extraordinarily scenic because of the indented coast and offshore islets.

For a country where sandy beaches are rare, it's unusual to find three very close to each other – and on a relatively small island. At Mljet's southernmost point is an oddly shaped peninsula, into which one of its many indents is **Limuni** beach (or Uvala Blaće). Fingers of pine forests arc protectively around the beach of fine sand, which has a long shallow section of clear blue-green water. It can be reached by road, even if the last part of it isn't paved.

Slightly more accessible is **Saplunara**. You won't find many facilities here, but you will find Aleppo pines and two beaches of soft sand. There's also a shingle beach closer to the centre. The village itself is very small (population approximately 32), but it does offer a few guesthouses and private rooms as well as campsites.

As you make your way across the island to the National Park, stop in **Babino Polje**, the island's largest village. You could check out the 15th-century church of St Blaise (Sv. Vlaho) and the 16th-century Ducal Palace at the edge of the village. A sign, Odisejeva špilja, directs you down a steep path to Odysseus' Cave where the great wanderer supposedly met Calypso, daughter of Atlas, during his lengthy voyage. Fearless locals make use of the raised shoreline around the cave and jump straight into the sparkling blue water and swim into the grotto. There are lower points from which to jump if you're not quite so fearless.

If you don't have a car, the public bus service is patchy at best. There are buses that connect the two ferry ports, but they're on a very limited schedule and not particularly reliable. Another option is to hire a scooter, which is cheaper and often more practical.

Food and Drink

① RESTAURANT MELITA

Otok Sv. Marija; tel: 020-744 145; daily 10am–midnight; €€

Vegetables are fresh from the monastery garden, and eggs are fresh from their chickens. The dishes are simple but tasty, and the shady terrace dining room makes you want to while away the day here.

② BARBE IVE

Pomena 4; tel: 098-669 662; www.kono babarbaive.com; daily 9am–midnight; €€

For fish so fresh it still twitches, try this friendly waterfront restaurant for seafood risotto, octopus stew and other excellent seafood dishes. Meat-eaters are catered for too, with plenty of hearty options.

Ston's lengthy 14th-century wall

PELJEŠAC PENINSULA

This one-day tour of the Pelješac wine-growing peninsula, Croatia's second-largest peninsula, includes a visit to the Ston wall, swimming on Trstenica Bay, lunch in Orebić, winery visits and dinner at Mali Ston.

DISTANCE: 226km (140 miles)
TIME: A full day
START/END: Dubrovnik
POINTS TO NOTE: You will need a car, as there are only one or two buses a day between Dubrovnik and Orebić. Visit the walls of Ston in the cool early morning. Pick up a map of the Pelješac wine road at the tourist office in Ston.

Separated from the mainland by a narrow channel, the Pelješac peninsula is a sparsely populated, mountainous sliver of land 71km (44 miles) long and 7km (4 miles) at its widest. The northeast part of the peninsula is scrubland, but the southwest is carpeted with fruit trees and vineyards that produce Pelješac's renowned Dingač and Postup wines. Equally renowned are the sandy beaches of the Pelješac peninsula – a rarity in Croatia.

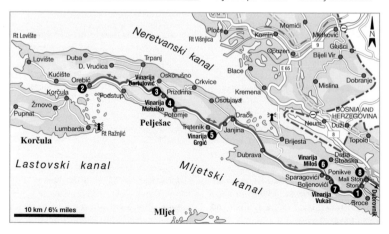

Mali Ston fisherman

STON

Leave Dubrovnik early in the morning and take the E65 coastal road to **Ston** ❶ (55km/34 miles). This appealing stone town is protected by a sturdy wall that winds up and around the hillside for 5km (3 miles), encircling Ston and neighbouring Mali Ston. In fact, the wall came before the towns. The Ragusa Republic (see page 82) annexed the region for its salt, and in the 14th century built walls to protect its investment. An irregular pentagon with massive corner towers fortifies the town, and the walls climb to the top of Podzvizd hill before descending to merge with the walls of Mali Ston. The wall system includes 40 towers and five forts. It's the longest fortification in Europe, and if you climb to the top you will be rewarded with sweeping views of the peninsula and the salt pans that are still in use today.

You can take a break in one of the cafés along Ston's **central square**.

OREBIĆ

Leave Ston and drive to **Orebić** ❷ (58km/36 miles), a rapidly developing coastal town with regular ferries across the channel to Korčula. Until the 19th century, Orebić was a major maritime centre; now it is famous for the beautiful pine-lined beach along **Trstenica Bay** at the eastern end of the town. It has some snack bars, or you can walk along the coast towards town, where you will find restaurants and cafés.

WINERIES

After lunch, head back east on the same road to visit some wineries. Most are family-run affairs and there's usually no need to book ahead, but some are closed at lunchtime. First up is **Vinarija Bartulović** ❸ (tel: 020-742 506; www.vinarijabartulovic.hr), a 480-year-old winery at Prizdrina. Next is **Vinarija Matuško** ❹ (tel: 020-742 399) in Potomje, which also serves food. Then it's on to the most famous (and expensive) winery, **Vinarija Grgić** ❺ (tel: 020-748 090; www.grgic-vina.com), at Trstenik, the Croatian branch of Grgić's California wine operation. **Vinarija Miloš** ❻ (tel: 098-965 6880; www.milos.hr) in Ponikve and **Vinarija Vukas** ❼ (tel: 098-203 012; www.vinavukas.com) in Boljenovići are two further options before reaching Ston.

MALI STON

Pass through Ston, and after a short way turn left to the tiny walled village of **Mali Ston** ❽. Croatians travel a good distance to feast on the seafood here. If you want to do the same, stop at **Kapetanova Kuća** (see ❶) before heading back to Dubrovnik.

Food and Drink

❶ **KAPETANOVA KUĆA**
Mali Ston; tel: 020-754 555; www.ostrea. hr; daily lunch and dinner; €€€
Sensational seafood on the waterfront.

Walled Korčula Town

KORČULA

The forested island of Korčula is famous for its olive oil and wine.
Tour the turrets, towers and churches of walled Korčula Town, then
relax on the sandy beaches of Lumbarda and taste the local Grk wine.

DISTANCE: Driving: 230km (140 miles); walking: 1km (0.5 mile)
TIME: A full day
START: Sea Gate
END: Large Governor's Tower
POINTS TO NOTE: In July and August there are regular morning catamarans (www.gv-line.hr) from Dubrovnik's Gruž harbour, west of the Old Town, that return in the afternoon. Tickets go on sale at the dock one hour before departure. The rest of the year you would need to hire a car, drive 115km (70 miles) to Orebić on the Pelješac peninsula, then make a 15-minute ferry crossing. You could then spend the night here and perhaps combine the trip with a visit to the Pelješac peninsula (see page 92). Once you have arrived at Korčula, be sure to check return ferry times.

Traces of Korčula's former Venetian overlords are readily apparent, from the ornate Renaissance flourishes on building façades to the paintings by Venetian artists in the cathedral. It remained under Venetian rule from 1420 to 1797, during which time the Venetians made good use of the local stone. Korčula was also an important shipbuilding centre. At their height, the island's shipyards rivalled those of Venice and Dubrovnik, and at the end of the 18th century there were still about 100 in operation.

KORČULA TOWN

As you approach Korčula by boat, the walled town's four sturdy towers, honey-coloured walls and terracotta roofs resemble a fairy-tale city. Once in harbour you will see straight ahead of you a broad flight of steps, dividing around a central fountain. This is the **Sea Gate ❶** (Primorska vrata), one of two entrances to the Old Town. Before going in you may like to pop into the adjacent **tourist office** (Obala Franje Tuđmana; tel: 020-725 701), which is set in a splendid 16th-century loggia. The terrace of the Hotel Korčula next door is an inviting place for a coffee.

Tintoretto alterpiece, St Mark's Cathedral

At the top of the steps is a terrace lined with café tables, and, straight ahead, a narrow alley (Ulica Dinka Miroševića) leads up to **Trg sv. Marka ❷** (St Mark's Square), where you will find the cathedral, the Treasury Museum and the Town Museum.

St Mark's Cathedral

Like most of Korčula's buildings, the Gothic-Renaissance **St Mark's Cathedral** (Katedrala sv. Marka; open daylight hours; free) is constructed from the mellow limestone that made the island – and its stone masters – prosperous and famous. The tower and cupola, dating from around 1480, are the work of Marko Andrjić, whose sons, Petar and Josip, worked on numerous prestigious buildings in Dubrovnik, including the Sponza Palace and the Rector's Palace. Flanking the main doorway are curly-maned lions and some rather lewd naked figures representing Adam and Eve. Above the door sits St Mark, robed as a bishop.

Inside, the cathedral is notable for a splendid high wooden ceiling; a huge stone canopy, also the work of Marko Andrjić, and built to his own design; and a richly coloured Tintoretto altarpiece (1550), depicting *St Mark with St Bartholomew and St Jerome*. In the south aisle there is an *Annunciation* that is ascribed to the School of Tintoretto; and in the north aisle there is Ivan Meštrovic's early 20th-century bronze statue of St Blaise (Sv. Vlaho).

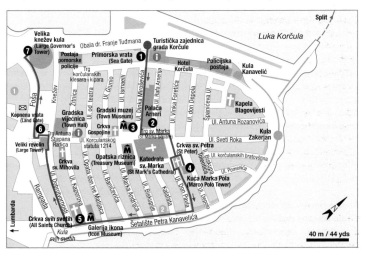

The Marco Polo Tower, behind St Peter's Church

Treasury Museum

To the right of the cathedral is the **Treasury Museum** (Opatska riznica; daily 9am–2pm, 5–8pm; charge). Its artworks range from 15th-century sacred paintings – including a precious polyptych of *Our Lady of Conception* by Blaž Trogiranin, one of the most respected 15th-century Dalmatian artists – to Ivan Meštrović's 20th-century bronze *Pietà*. There are also ecclesiastical robes, chalices and processional crucifixes; at ground level there's a cool kitchen, with large metal pots in the hearth and shelves stacked with Roman pots that were recovered from the sea in the 1960s.

Town Museum

Directly opposite is the **Town Museum** ❸ (Gradski muzej; July–Sept 9am–9pm, Apr–June 10am–2pm, Oct–Mar 10am–1pm; charge), in a Renaissance palace built for the wealthy Gabrielis family in the 16th century. The ground floor has an interesting exhibition on the island's stonemasons; the first floor concentrates on Korčula's second important industry, shipbuilding. Elsewhere in the museum are rooms housing 17th- to 19th-century furniture, elaborate costumes, and kitchen implements. On the top floor are photographs of Tito's Partisans, including one showing the First Conference of the People's Liberation Council for the district, held in November 1943, along with an old typewriter used by the Partisans.

Marco Polo Tower

Leave the square at the northern corner, taking Ulica sv. Roka. The first street on your right is Ulica Depolo, the alleged location of Marco Polo's birthplace. While most historians agree that Marco Polo was born in Venice, the people of Korčula claim the explorer as a member of the local Depolo family. The lovely **Marco Polo Tower** ❹ (Kuća Marka Pola; daily 9am–8pm; charge), entered through a pretty vine-covered patio, with stunning views from the top, forms part of what is claimed to be the Depolo family home. The attached building – a graceful, ruined Gothic palace – is now the **Marco Polo Museum** (open July–Aug 9am–9pm, Apr–Jun, Oct 9am–3pm; charge), with life-size exhibits re-creating Polo's exploits.

Church of All Saints and Icon Museum

From the Church of St Peter take the steps down Ulica Don Pavla to Šetalište Petra Kanavelića and turn right. At the end of the road you will come to the **Church of All Saints** ❺ (Crkva svih svetih; usually open in daylight hours; free) in order to see a beautiful 15th-century polyptych by Blaž Trogiranin. Across the way is the **Icon Museum** (Galerija ikona; daily 10am–2pm and 5–7pm; charge), housed in the Hall of the Brotherhood of All Saints. Painted on wood in tempera and gilt, some of the 17th- and 18th-century icons are truly exquisite.

Sea Gate detail

The Land Gate

Gates and towers

Continue on Ulica Dobrotvornosti on the other side of the church and you will come to the majestic stone steps leading to the **Land Gate ❻** (Kopnena vrata) to the town. On the left is the 15th-century **Large Tower** (Veliki revelin) and ahead is the **Town Hall** (Gradska vijećnica). Climb the tower for far-reaching views of the glistening sea and the coastline.

Afterwards go down the steps out of the Old Town and turn right, until you reach the cone-shaped **Large Governor's Tower ❼** (Velika knežev kula). This was built at the western corner of the walls to protect both the Governor's Palace (now demolished) and the harbour. Turn left here, and follow the harbour road for a different view of Korčula and the chance to swim at one of two small bathing beaches. Alternatively, carry on along Ulica Plokata for a simple lunch at **Konoba Škver** (see ❶).

LUMBARDA

Korčula is more than just a town; there's a whole island to explore. If you have a car, you could take the main road to Vela Luka to explore the forested interior. But even without a car, it is worth taking a look at Lumbarda, 6km (4 miles) southeast of Korčula Town. There are hourly buses (make sure to check the return schedule at Korčula's bus station), or you could hire a taxi or a taxi boat from the eastern harbour on the way to the bus station. En route, you will pass acres of vineyards growing the Grk grape to make Lumbarda's renowned white wine.

Lumbarda itself is a pleasant and low-key small town on a harbour and endowed with the island's best beaches. Walk south out of town for 1km (0.75 mile) to come to two sandy beaches: Pržina and Bilin Žal. The fine sand and shallow water make either one suitable for kids. On your return to Lumbarda you could sample some local wine at one of the harbourside cafés. For dinner back in Korčula Town, settle on the quayside terrace of **Restaurant Filippi** (see ❷).

Food and Drink

❶ KONOBA ŠKVER

Plokata 19; tel: 020-716 5224; daily 8am–midnight; €

For a relaxed lunch – or a hearty mid-morning *marenda*, rather like brunch – sit in the cosy stone interior or the patio of this friendly restaurant.

❷ RESTAURANT FILIPPI

Šetalište Petra Kanavelića; tel: 020-711 690; www.restaurantfilippi.com; daily 9am–midnight; €€

Modern Dalmatian cuisine mixes with Italian influences in this classy waterside restaurant overlooking the Pelješac peninsula, where only fish that's been caught locally will appear on the menu.

DIRECTORY

Hand-picked hotels and restaurants to suit all budgets and tastes,
organised by area, plus select nightlife listings, an alphabetical
listing of practical information, a language guide and an overview
of the best books and films to give you a flavour of the country.

Pool at the DoubleTree

ACCOMMODATION

Croatia's hotels are often sprawling structures, built during the tourist boom of the 1970s. However, in the past few years, many have undergone major overhauls. The hotel scene is definitely upwardly mobile, with more luxury and boutique hotels opening each year.

Hotel categories use the standard international grading system. Prices vary according to the season and are up to 50 percent less off-season. For stays of less than three days you may have to pay a surcharge. Prices are posted in euros; you may pay in kuna or euros if you pay in cash. Breakfast is usually included in the price.

There is a tourist tax charged on every stay, whether you stay in hotel or private accommodation. The tax is per person and per night, but it varies according to the location and the season. It runs between about 2.20Kn and 7Kn.

Unlike hotels along the coast, the prices of Zagreb hotels stay the same all year round. Many hotels cater to business travellers and tend to fill up during fairs and conferences.

Agrotourism, which offers accommodation in rural properties and farms, is a great option for families with children. So far it has only really taken off in Istria, but it is developing in Dalmatia.

On the islands, private rooms (most with self-catering facilities and en-suite bathrooms) are a good bet, and hosts are very welcoming and hospitable. There are hundreds of agencies handling accommodation rentals in Croatia. A good place to start is the Croatia National Tourist Board website, www.croatia.hr. If you arrive without a reservation, head to the local tourist office or look for signs saying *sobe* (rooms).

Most campsites are open May–Sept, although a few operate all year. They range from large autocamps with loads of facilities to smaller camps in pretty locations. A good online guide is www.camping.hr.

Zagreb

Arcotel Allegra
Branimirova 29; tel: 01-469 6000; www.arcotelhotels.com; €€€

This Austrian-owned design hotel is centrally located, offers spacious rooms and a Mediterranean-styled restaurant. There's a wellness centre with a whirlpool and a gym. The hotel is great value if you manage get one of the online deals when booking.

Price for two people sharing a double room in peak season:
€€€€ = over 220 euros
€€€ = 160–220 euros
€€ = 90–160 euros
€ = below 90 euros

Room at the Esplanade Zagreb Hotel

DoubleTree by Hilton

Grada Vukovara 269a; tel: 01-600 1900; www.doubletree.com; €€€

The upmarket Hilton offshoot is in the centre of the Green Gold business district. The plush, contemporary rooms are spacious and stylish, and there's a spa with an indoor pool and a gym.

Hotel Dubrovnik

Ljudivita Gajeva 1; tel: 01-486 3503; www.hotel-dubrovnik.hr; €€

Clad in mirrored glass, the four-star Hotel Dubrovnik is in a perfect location just off Trg Jelačića. Many of the rooms have a view of the square, and the double-glazed windows are effective at keeping out the noise.

Esplanade Zagreb Hotel

Mihanovićeva 1; tel: 01-456 6666; www.esplanade.hr; €€€€

Built in 1925 for passengers of the Orient Express, the five-star Esplanade stands next to the station. The swirl of marble in the lobby gives a taste of the classical splendour of the rooms. Modern facilities include a wellness centre and first-class dining.

Jägerhorn

Ilica 14; tel: 01-483 3877; www.hotel-jagerhorn.hr; €€

This historic hotel has been on this city-centre site since 1827. Its 18 stylish rooms are charming and bright, and there's a wonderful garden café – all just minutes away from Zagreb's main square.

Plitvice

Hotel Jezero

Velika Poljana; tel: 053-751 500; www.np-plitvicka-jezera.hr; €€

This large modern hotel includes an indoor pool and sauna. All rooms are bright and plushly decorated, but try to get one with a balcony and a lake view. The hotel is open all year round.

Hotel Plitvice

Velika Poljana; tel: 053-751 200; www.np-plitvicka-jezera.hr; €€

This is a very comfortable hotel, although the rooms are not quite as expensively fitted out as those at the Hotel Jezero next door. Still, there is ample heat or air-con depending on the season, but no pool.

Istria: Bale

Villa Meneghetti

Stancija Meneghetti; tel: 091-243 1600; www.meneghettiinfo.com; €€€€

This secluded villa in the heart of a vineyard is pure class. There are only four rooms in this Relais & Châteaux hotel, all of them in chic country-cottage style. There's also a top-notch restaurant, indoor and outdoor pools and glorious countryside.

Istria: Poreč

Hotel Laguna Parentium

Zelena Laguna; tel: 052-411 500;

The Hotel Monte Mulini enjoys a stunning waterfront setting

www.lagunaporec.com; €€€

Sitting on a peninsula fringed by pine groves, this classy four-star 5km (3 miles) from Poreč has two pools and its own beach. It's mainly geared towards adults who want to spoil themselves in lush surroundings, with sea views and balconies.

Hotel Mauro

Obala M. Tita 15; tel: 052-219 500; www.hotelmauro.com; €€€

This smart boutique four-star is in a fantastic location right on the waterfront, and some of the contemporary rooms have balconies with sea views. The waterfront restaurant terrace is a bonus.

Hotel Poreč

Rade Končara 1; tel: 052-451 811; www.hotelporec.com; €

This comfortable low-cost hotel next door to the bus station is a great favourite with backpackers and budget travellers, which lends the hotel a most convivial atmosphere. Rooms are well maintained and spacious, with modern bathrooms. It is only a 10-minute walk to all the attractions of Poreč.

Hotel Valamar Diamant

Brulo bb; tel: 052-400 000; www.valamar.com; €€€€

This vast modern hotel has excellent sports facilities that include indoor and outdoor swimming pools and 16 tennis courts. There is also an impressive health and beauty centre. It's a 20-minute walk from the Old Town and open all year.

Istria: Rovinj

Casa Garzotto

Ulica Grisia 8; tel: 052-811 884; www.casagarzotto.com; €€

Five separate Venetian buildings make up this charming boutique hotel in the centre of Rovinj. Rooms have cosy traditional furnishings, and some apartments are available. Classic Istrian dishes are served in the intimate restaurant.

Hotel Adriatic

Pina Budicina 2; tel: 052-800 250; www.maistra.com; €€€€

This stately four-star townhouse hotel right on the harbour had a major renovation and now has 18 stylish suites with original works of art. There's also a French-style brasserie with a waterside terrace.

Island Hotel Katarina

Otok sv. Katarine; tel: 052-800 250; www.maistra.com; €€–€€€€

This large hotel is on St Katherine's Island, a short shuttle boat away from Rovinj. It is a great option for families, with plenty of facilities including a pool and tennis. Outside July and August, the room rate plunges considerably.

Hotel Lone

Luje Adamovića; tel: 052-800 250;

Villa Angelo d'Oro

www.lonehotel.com; €€€€
This five-star design hotel brings a sleek modern look to the depths of the Zlatni Rt forest park. Smartly furnished rooms are spacious and have balconies from which take in the forest views. There's an indoor pool and spa too.

Hotel Monte Mulini
Antonia Smareglia 3; tel: 052-636 000; www.montemulinihotel.com; €€€€€
A member of the Leading Hotels of the World, this five-star luxury hotel is a more intimate version of its neighbour Hotel Lone (also owned by Maistra). Its contemporary rooms have terraces with views of the Zlatni Rt forest park, and guests can use the Lone's spa if they want a change from the Monte Mulini's own excellent wellness facilities.

Villa Angelo d'Oro
Via Švalbe 38–42; tel: 052-853 920; www.angelodoro.com; €€€–€€€€
This luxury hotel occupies a restored 17th-century bishop's palace in the Old Town. The design is imaginative but still respects the traditional setting. All the rooms are individually furnished with antiques, and there's a very charming courtyard garden.

Istria: Pula

Hotel Scaletta
Flavijevska 26; tel: 052-541 599; www.hotel-scaletta.com; €
For a little more style in the centre of town, try this attractive family-run hotel. Rooms

are somewhat small, but the cheerful decor makes up for the lack of space. The tastefully restored town house is just a stone's throw from the Arena.

Hotel Valsabbion
Pješčana uvala IX/26, Medulin; tel: 052-522 991; www.valsabbion.net; €€€
This lovingly constructed and furnished boutique hotel not only has an award-winning restaurant but also beautifully designed contemporary rooms. Overlooking the sea, 4km (2.5 miles) from the city centre, it offers a beauty centre and hydro-massage pool, plus a fitness centre.

Park Plaza Histria
Verudela; tel: 052-590 000; www.parkplaza.com; €€€
Although built for mass tourism decades ago, this hotel on the Verudela peninsula has been extremely well maintained. The full resort experience includes several large saltwater pools, a wellness centre and water sports such as water-skiing, scuba-diving and banana boats.

Villa Vulin
Tommaseova 10; tel: 052-393 990; www.villa-vulin.hr; €€€€
South of the Old Town but only a 10-minute walk from the sea, this charming hotel lives up to its 'boutique' label: it has only six suites. All are spacious and handsomely furnished, some with large terraces with sea views.

The sea view at Le Méridien Lav

Central Dalmatia: Split

Hotel Peristil

Poljana kraljice Jelene 5; tel: 021-329 070; www.hotelperistil.com; €€

This is an excellent-value hotel with a spectacular location in Diocletian's Palace. Only some rooms have a view of the Peristyle, but all have soothing interior design and some incorporate parts of the ancient walls. Despite the busy location, rooms are soundproof.

Le Méridien Lav

Grljevačka 2a, Podstrana; tel: 021-500 500; www.lemeridienlavsplit.com; €€€€

Podstrana is 8km (5 miles) south of town, but Le Méridien Lav is a complete resort with spa, casino, restaurants, infinity pools and a private beach. Rooms are airy and modern, with sea views and balconies.

Vestibul Palace

Iza Vestibula 4a; tel: 021-329 329; www.vestibulpalace.com; €€€€

Much thought and expense were put into this upmarket hotel set in Diocletian's Palace. Luxurious rooms have handcrafted leather furnishings and sleek designs that suit the exposed stone walls beautifully. While it's pricey, there are some off-season bargains to be had.

Zephyrus Boutique Accommodation

Milićeva 5; tel: 098-998 6597; www.zephyrus.hr; €€€–€€€€

In the depths of Diocletian's Palace is this chic spot mixing rooms with apartments – all designed with flair. Both apartments have fully equipped kitchen, and one has a terrace with wonderful views of the city.

Central Dalmatia: Trogir

Villa Pape

Marinova Draga 30; tel: 021-460 410; www.villa-pape.com; €

The English-speaking owners of this relaxing, family-run guesthouse on Čiovo island go out of their way to make guests feel welcome. Excellent home-cooked meals make it worthwhile to take half-board. Modern rooms are comfortable and air-conditioned.

Villa Sikaa

Obala kralja Zvonimira 10; tel: 021-881 223; www.vila-sikaa-r.com; €€

Located just outside the Old Town, Villa Sikaa offers modern rooms and friendly service. Most rooms have sea views, and there's one with a balcony. The owners can also arrange scooter or car hire through their own travel agency.

Central Dalmatia: Šibenik

Hotel Life Palace

Trg Šibeniskih Palih Boraca 1; tel: 022-219 005; www.hotel-lifepalace.hr; €€€€

The amenities are modern but the mood is decidedly Baroque in this lavishly restored Renaissance palace in the heart of the city. Exposed stone walls

and ceiling beams add to the romantic atmosphere. Some of the rooms have balconies overlooking the restaurant terrace below.

Central Dalmatia: Makarska

Boutique Hotel Marco Polo
Obala 15, Gradac; tel: 021-695 060; www.hotel-marcopolo.com; €€€€
This smart boutique hotel is on the seafront at Gradac, with contemporary rooms (some with balconies and sea views). The beach is right out front, but there's also an outdoor pool and a roof terrace with sun loungers.

Hotel Biokovo
Obala Kralja Tomislava bb; tel: 021-615 244; www.holidaymakarska.com; €€
Situated on the seafront just 150m/yds from the town's pebble beach, this is a decent hotel in a charming location. Ask for a room with a balcony to enjoy the views.

Central Dalmatia: Vis

Hotel Biševo
Ribarska 72, Komiža; tel: 021-713 279; hotel-bisevo.com.hr; €
The rooms are functional in this large hotel, but its best asset is its location right on the beach between the woods and Komiža town. Rooms have balconies, and most have sea views.

Hotel Issa
Šetalište Zanelle 5; tel: 021-711 164; hotelsvis.hr; €€

With 125 rooms, Hotel Issa is larger than its sister hotel, the Tamaris, but is more down at heel. It's on the western part of Vis harbour in a more modern building. Ask for a room with a sea view.

Hotel San Giorgio
Petra Hektorovića; tel: 021-711 362; www.hotelsangiorgiovis.com; €€€
Vis's best hotel – tucked away in a charming alleyway – has attractive, individually decorated rooms, some with balconies and whirlpool baths. There's a fine restaurant, and even the chance to stay in a lighthouse on a separate island.

Hotel Tamaris
Obala sv. Jurja 30; tel: 021-711 164; www.hotelsvis.com; €€
It may be quite basic and in need of an update, but this three-star hotel is housed in an attractive, late 19th-century building overlooking Vis harbour. There's also a lovely waterfront restaurant.

Central Dalmatia: Hvar

Hidden House
Duoljno Kola 13; tel: 091-266 4444; www.hidden-house.com; €–€€
British couple Chris and Amanda have turned a 300-year-old stone house in Stari Grad into a sumptuous and chic B&B. There are only four rooms, each individually decorated in an imaginative, elegant and supremely comfort-

Junior suite at the Riva Hvar Yacht Harbor Hotel

able style that makes the most of the exposed stone walls. The roof terrace is a treat.

Hotel Park Hvar

Blankete bb; tel: 021-718 337; www.hotelparkhvar.com; €€€–€€€€

This homely hotel in a 16th-century house is right in the centre of town, and many of its spacious and airy rooms have exposed stone walls and balconies overlooking the harbour. Some of the rooms have separate sitting rooms.

Hotel Podstine

Put Podstina 11; tel: 021-740 400; www.podstine.com; €€€€

This secluded, family-run hotel is a 20-minute walk along the coast from town and set in spectacular surroundings. Ask for a room with a balcony, preferably facing the sea. Spa facilities include an outdoor pool.

Riva Hvar Yacht Harbor Hotel

Obala Riva 27; tel: 021-750 750; www.suncanihvar.hr; €€€€

This waterfront boutique hotel offers artfully designed rooms with a Hollywood theme on the promenade in the heart of Hvar Town's lively nightlife. Its terrace restaurant is one of the trendiest in town.

Southern Dalmatia: Dubrovnik

Dubrovnik President

Iva Dulčića 39; tel: 020-441 100; www.valamar.com; €€€€

Classy and beautifully decorated, the five-star Dubrovnik President has what may be Dubrovnik's best beach, a well-maintained stretch of smooth pebbles on a quiet cove in Babin Kuk. All the rooms have large terraces with sweeping views of the sea.

Fresh Sheets

Bunićeva Poljana 6; tel: 091-799 2086; www.freshsheetsbedandbreakfast.com; €€€

Croatian-Canadian couple Jon and Sanja runs this friendly B&B next to the cathedral in the Old Town, offering smartly furnished rooms and the personal touch. Save room for the large made-to-order breakfasts.

Grand Villa Argentina

Put Frana Supila 14; tel: 020-440 555; www.adriaticluxuryhotels.com; €€€€

Surrounded by pine trees in a beautiful setting that's only a five-minute walk from the Old Town, this five-star luxury hotel has a private beach, indoor and outdoor pools as well as stylish rooms with sublime views.

Hotel Splendid

Masarykov Put 10; tel: 020-433 560; www.dubrovnikhotels.travel; €€€

Situated on the Lapad peninsula at the edge of a small, private cove, this is a good mid-range choice. Rooms are spacious, if somewhat lacking in decorative flourishes. All rooms are

Room with a view at Villa Dubrovnik

quiet, but try to get a room overlooking the sea.

Hotel Vis

Masarykov Put 4; tel: 020-433 555; www.dubrovnikhotels.travel; €€

Right on the Lapad peninsula, this large hotel is ideal for families. The decor needs updating, but the beach is close and the restaurant terrace has wonderful views. Upgrade to a room with a balcony and sea view.

Hotel Zagreb

Šetalište Kralje Zonimira 27; tel: 020-438 930; www.hotelzagreb-dubrovnik.com; €€

This traditional hotel is in an attractive terracotta-coloured building set in palm-shaded gardens. Rooms have quite a straightforward decor, but the hotel is an easy walk to Lapad's beach and it's just as easy to catch a bus to the Old Town.

Prijeko Palace

Prijeko 22; tel: 020-321 145; www.prijekopalace.com; €€€€

This sumptuous nine-room boutique hotel in Prijeko is a riot of colour and Baroque splendour, thanks to the original works created by contemporary artists. The roof terrace has fantastic views of the Old Town.

St Joseph's

Svetog Josipa 3; tel: 020-432 089; www.stjosephs.hr; €€€€

This elegant and intimate boutique hotel is in a 500-year-old house in a quiet lane off Stradun. Its six rooms are in a refined French country cottage style and come with sleek modern kitchens.

Stari Grad

Od Sigurate 4; tel: 020-322 244; www.hotelstarigrad.com; €€€€

Just off Stradun is this smart boutique hotel with only eight rooms furnished in a contemporary style. Its roof terrace restaurant has wonderful views and food to match.

Villa Dubrovnik

Vlaha Bukovka 6; tel: 021-500 300; www.villa-dubrovnik.hr; €€€€

The setting is incomparable in this high-end cliff-top hotel with an indoor/outdoor pool and a private beach. One of the Leading Hotels of the World, this sumptuous hotel has a roof terrace with some of the city's best views.

Vila Mičika

Mata Vodopića 10; tel: 020-437 332; www.vilamicika.hr; €

This simple budget hotel is handy for Lapad's beaches. It's very basic and functional, but the rooms have their own bathrooms and all have the use of a shared kitchen on each floor.

Villa Wolff

Nika i Meda Pucica 1; tel: 021-438 710; www.villa-wolff.hr; €€€

The infinity pool at Boutique Pine Tree Resort

This boutique hotel is in a busy part of Lapad, but manages to create a quiet atmosphere for its guests. Rooms are attractively decorated, and some have private terraces with a view of the sea, which is right below.

Southern Dalmatia: Cavtat

Hotel Supetar
Ante Starčevića 27; tel: 020-479 833; www.adriaticluxuryhotels.com; €€€

The friendly Supetar is right by the bay in a traditional stone building. Its comfortably furnished 28 rooms have views either of the bustling waterfront or the tranquil garden. Its roof terrace is a superb place for breakfast and dinner.

Remisens Hotel Albatross
Od Žala 1; tel: 051-710 444; www.reminsens.com; €€€

This sprawling family-friendly hotel is right by the beach, and has indoor and outdoor pools and plenty of activities for children. Rooms are functionally furnished, but all come with balconies. There's also an all-inclusive option.

Villa Pattiera
Trumbićev put 9; tel: 020-478 800; www.villa-pattiera.hr; €€€

The birthplace of the Croatian tenor Tino Pattiera is a cosy boutique hotel by the harbour. All 12 rooms have either a shared balcony or terrace, and the hotel also runs the Dalmacija restaurant across the road.

Southern Dalmatia: Koločep

Sensimar Kalamota Island Resort
Donje Čelo; tel: 020-312 150; www.karismaadriatic.om; €€€€

What had been the Hotel Villas Koločep has been turned into an adults-only, all-inclusive luxury resort overlooking Donje Čelo Bay. Modern rooms come with balconies, and there's a pool as well as a beach in front of the resort.

Southern Dalmatia: Mljet

Boutique Accommodation Mljet
Goveđari 14; tel: 020-744 140; www.boutiqueaccommodationmljet.com; €–€€

In the heart of the National Park are these three homely apartments, complete with beamed ceilings, comfortable traditional furniture and full kitchens. One has a dreamy loggia with wonderful views of the woods.

Boutique Pine Tree Resort
Saplunara 17; tel: 098-266 007; www.boutiquepinetree.com; €€€€

Stealing a march on the island's only official hotel is this very stylish apartment hotel overlooking the sea. It's much pricier, but the attractive apartments all come with terraces and kitchens. There's an infinity pool as well as a restaurant, and the beach is a stone's throw away.

Presidential suite at the Radisson Blu Resort

Hotel Odisej
Pomena; tel: 020-744 022;
www.adriaticluxuryhotels.com; €€

Mljet's only official hotel is on the northern side of the island in Pomena, just outside the entrance to the national park. The rooms are in great need of updating, and it's definitely worth getting a balcony with a sea view. The restaurant terrace is lovely, however.

Southern Dalmatia: Korčula

Hotel Korčula
Obala Franjo Tuđmana; tel: 020-711 078;
€€€

Some of the rooms are on the small side in this three-star hotel, but the Old Town location right by the water is excellent. There's also a vine-shaded terrace and a good restaurant with a popular café.

Lešić Dimitri Palace
Don Pavla Pose 1-6; tel: 020-715 560;
www.ldpalace.com; €€€€

Set in an 18th-century bishop's palace in the heart of the Old Town is this chic Relais & Châteaux boutique hotel. Its opulent rooms hark back to the days of the Silk Road, with suitably oriental touches.

Marko Polo Hotel
Šetalište Frana Kršića 102; tel: 020-726 336; €€€

Located on a hill outside Korčula Town, the Marko Polo has quite standard rooms – most with balconies – but the views of the town make up for it. There's an outdoor pool, and it's only a short walk to the beach.

Pansion Bebić
Lumbarda; tel: 020-712 505; www.bebic.hr; €

Those eager to experience a more authentic Korčula should try Pansion Bebić. The multilingual Bebić family has welcomed guests for years and add a personal touch to everything, from the well-appointed rooms to the delicious meals served on their delightful terrace-restaurant.

Southern Dalmatia: Mali Ston

Hotel Vila Koruna
Peljeski put 1; tel: 020-754 999; €

Famous as Mali Ston's oldest restaurant, the Vila Koruna has functional rooms including two apartments. The main draw is the restaurant serving local oysters – preferably on the large terrace overlooking the bay.

Southern Dalmatia: Orašac

Radisson Blu Resort
Na Moru 1; tel: 020-361 500;
www.radissonblu.com; €€€€

It's unabashed luxury at this contemporary, cliff-hugging resort 11km (7 miles) west of Dubrovnik, with an enormous spa, infinity pool and its own marina. During the seasons, there's a boat shuttle to the Old Town.

Alfresco drinks in Zagreb Old Town

RESTAURANTS

Croatians place a strong priority on eating well and expect restaurants to reach a high standard of quality. There is not yet much of a taste for exotic food, so there is a certain sameness to the menus. Fish is almost always grilled in olive oil, garlic and lemon juice. Black risotto is on nearly every menu along the coast, and the main vegetable is likely to be *blitva* (swiss chard). Restaurants in Zagreb and, recently, in Dubrovnik tend to be more adventurous – and expensive.

Do not be surprised to see an additional 7–10Kn on your bill at the end the meal. It is the 'bread charge' that appears whether or not you ate the bread. Restaurants are supposed to indicate this supplement on the menu, but some do not. If you pay in cash you may be able to get the restaurant to waive the charge.

While Croatians are in the habit of dressing neatly wherever they go, they have a generally relaxed attitude that makes them reluctant to enforce picky dress codes and rules. There-fore, you will rarely encounter a dress code to enter any but the most exclusive restaurants. You will feel more in the swing, however, if you dress 'smart casual' at night.

Some restaurants in resort areas won't be open all year round, generally closing from October to April. The times are rarely fixed, however, as the season can be quite elastic depending on the weather and the whim of the restaurateur.

Zagreb: Upper Town

Agava

Tkalčićeva 39; tel: 01-482 9826; www.restaurant-agava.hr; daily 9am–11pm; €€€

There's a pleasing mix of Mediterranean flavours in this relaxed restaurant that manages to be cosy despite its rather sprawling size. French and Italian flavours easily mingle with Croatian, and the terrace is a great place to watch all the action on Tkalčićeva while you're dining.

Dubravkin Put

Dubravkin Put 2; tel: 01-483 4975; Mon–Sat 11am–1am; €€€€

This is one of the best fish restaurants in town. The setting is exquisite, on the edge of Tušanac Park. In fine weather it is a pleasure to enjoy your meal on a leafy terrace. In cooler weather, you can

> Price guide for an average meal for two, with a glass of house wine:
> €€€€ = over 440Kn
> €€€ = 330–440Kn
> €€ = 220–330Kn
> € = below 220Kn

A cold platter for lunch

appreciate the modern art decorating the elegant dining room.

Kaptolska Klet

Kaptol 5; tel: 01-487 6502; www.kaptolska-klet.eu; daily 11am–midnight; €€

Kaptolska Klet is a vast, welcoming space opposite the cathedral offering a robust Zagorje menu. Most dishes are hearty meat, but there are also lighter vegetarian dishes. During the summer there is a delightful beer garden to eat in.

Lanterna na Dolcu

Opatovina 31; tel: 01-481 9009; www.lanterna-zagreb.com; Tues–Sun 11am–10pm; €€

Snuggle under the brick vaulted ceiling in this convivial restaurant just beyond the cathedral. Classic Croatian dishes make up the menu, its freshness guaranteed by the wonderful produce bought in Dolac market.

Pod Gričkim Topom

Zakmardijeve Stube 5; tel: 01-483 3607; Mon–Sat 11am–midnight; €€

Up in Gornji grad, near the funicular station, this informal restaurant has the best location in the city, with fantastic views over the Lower Town. The good Croatian food equals the surroundings with an emphasis on generous portions of fish.

Restoran Nokturno

Skalinska 4; tel: 01-481 3394; www.restoran.nokturno.hr; Sun–Thur 8am–midnight, Fri–Sat 9am–1am; €

This cheerful and lively spot is just off Dolac market and has tables tucked into a raised terrace in the narrow street. It's a solid choice for incredibly cheap pizzas, risottos and local meat dishes.

Zagreb: Lower Town

OXBO Urban Bar & Grill

Ulica Grada Vukovara 269a; tel: 01-600 1914; www.oxbogrill.com; Mon–Fri 6.30am–11pm, Sat–Sun 7am–11pm; €€€

Steak-lovers in the Green Gold business district are well catered for in the DoubleTree Hilton's buzzing restaurant. It's a very classy space in which to enjoy the restaurant's speciality: juicy cuts of Black Angus beef.

Pivnica Medvedgrad

Ilica 49; tel: 01-4846 922; www.pivnica-medvedgrad.hr; daily 10am–midnight; €–€€

Home-made sausages, roast meats, grills, schnitzels and a range of good salads are complemented by a choice of craft beers that are brewed on the premises. The atmosphere is relaxed and jolly, especially in the large beer garden.

Stari Fijaker 900

Mesnička 6; tel: 01-483 3829; www.starifijaker.hr; Mon–Sat 11am–11pm, Sun 11am–10pm; €€

This traditional spot has long been a meeting place for artists, revolutionaries

Poreč boasts some excellent pizzerias

and family dinners since 1848, mainly because of the hearty Zagorje specialities prepared the way granny did. The menu includes all the staples of northern Croatian cuisine.

Vinodol
Nikole Tesle 10; tel. 01-481 1427; www.vinodol-zg.hr; daily 10am–midnight; €€

Choose from the large courtyard or the vaulted interior for well-cooked and reasonably priced traditional dishes. One of the stand-outs is succulent veal cooked under a *peka* so it just melts in the mouth.

Istria: Poreč

Istra
Bože Milanovića 30; tel: 052-434 636; daily noon–midnight; €€

Whether in the intimate dining rooms or on the terrace, you will feast well at this rustic establishment, popular with the locals. Try the lobster with noodles, cuttlefish *buzara* (in a tomato sauce) or fish *pod pekom* (cooked under a baking lid).

Konoba Ulixes
Decumanus 2; tel: 052-451 132; Mon–Sat noon–midnight; €€€

The Croatian dishes here are always served with a special touch. Taste seasonal products like asparagus or truffles, or try the unusual frogfish cooked in a seafood and prosecco sauce. The wine list focuses on the wonderful wines from Istria.

Pizzeria Dali
Istarskog razvoda 11; tel: 052-452 666; daily 11am–11pm; €

This small and traditional pizzeria serves excellent wood-fired pizzas as well as pasta dishes and grilled meats right in the heart of town. Inside it's all rustic and wooden, and there's a covered terrace for warm days.

Pizzeria Nono
Zagrebačka 4; tel: 052-453 088; daily noon–midnight; €

Whether it is because of the crowds of Italians flocking to the coast, or the fact that so many Croatians have worked in Italy, Croatian pizza can hold its own next to Italy's best. Even though there are savoury pasta dishes and hearty salads, most people come for the pizza.

Sarajevo Grill
Mlatka Vlačića; tel: 052-431 904; daily 9am–midnight; €€

Simple, tasty grilled meats and seafood are the speciality in this friendly, down-to-earth restaurant. You won't go hungry, nor will you end up spending much money if you stick to the cheaper meat dishes.

Sv. Nikola
Obala maršala Tita 23; tel: 052-423 018; www.svnikola.com; daily 9am–midnight; €€€

The dining is fine indeed in this elegant restaurant. There are two set menus: a fish menu that includes lobster, and

Backstreet restaurant in Rovinj

a meat menu that includes steak, but both are likely to include carpaccio and truffles in some form. It's highly popular with Italians, as truffles are much more expensive in Italy.

Istria: Rovinj

La Puntulina

Sv Križa 38; tel: 052-813 186; daily noon–midnight; €€€

It's hard to find a more romantic spot than this waterside restaurant with a terrace tumbling down towards the sea. The menu is classically Istrian, with plenty of perfectly grilled fish and seafood as well as meat dishes.

Scuba

Obala Pina Budicina 6; tel: 098-219 446; daily lunch and dinner; €€

Seafood is the star in this lively waterfront restaurant, where you can fill up on plentiful dishes of grilled fish, mussels, squid and other treats. There's also a good selection of typically Istrian pasta dishes if you're not a fan of seafood.

Istria: Pula

Kantina

Flantička 16; tel: 052-214 054; www.kantinapula.com; Mon–Sat 7am–midnight; €€

Dining in Pula's town centre offers few options, as most residents prefer to head out to the Verudela peninsula. Kantina is the best option in town. Steak with truffles, slow-cooked veal cheeks and mussel stew are popular dishes in this 19th-century building.

Oasi

Pješčana Uvala 10–12; tel: 052-317 910; daily noon–midnight; www.oasi.hr; €€€

The restaurant in the boutique hotel of the same name is a sophisticated spot on the coast about 6km (3.7 miles) south of Pula. There's an excellent mix of seafood, steaks and homemade pasta, with the expected smattering of Istrian truffles.

Vodnjaka Trattoria

Dinka Vitezića 4; tel: 098-175 7343; daily lunch and dinner; €€

It's a bit out of the way, but this simple trattoria is a friendly, family-run place that offers solid meat and seafood dishes – although vegetarians might have a problem. There's a cute little courtyard terrace too.

Istria: Vodnjan

Restoran Vodnjanka

Istarska bb; tel: 052-511 435; Mon–Sat lunch and dinner; €€

The rustic setting perfectly suits the rustic food with ingredients fresh from the Istrian countryside. Naturally there are truffles, but do not miss the wonderful asparagus when it is in season, as well as the homemade pasta and gnocchi.

Istria: Roč

Ročka Konoba

Roč; tel: 052-666 451; Tue–Sat lunch and

Restaurants and cafés line the Riva in Split

dinner; €€

This homespun restaurant serving is where Istrians come to when they want to get away from the coastal madness. Try the homemade Istrian sausages or *gulaš sa njokima* (goulash with gnocchi) with a glass of their homemade wine on the terrace.

Central Dalmatia: Split

Dvor
Put Firula 14; tel: 021-571 513; daily 8am–midnight; €€€

Head out of the Old Town to the west and you get a magical waterside setting on a stone terrace along with beautifully prepared food. The menu can be quite limited, but there's no doubting the quality of the seafood, pasta and risotto dishes.

Galija
Tončićeva 12; tel: 021-347 932; daily lunch and dinner; €€

Just outside Diocletian's Palace is this buzzing pizzeria that's more like a local pub. The pizza is excellent and comes from a wood-fired oven. It does get very busy, so it's not the place for a quiet lunch.

Kod Joze
Sredmanuška 4; tel: 021-347 397; daily lunch and dinner; €–€€

This typical *konoba* is just outside the palace walls, with good risotto, pasta and fish served either in a warm rustic interior or on a terrace in summer.

Locals love this place, perhaps because it's somewhat hidden from the tourist circuit.

Konoba Korta
Poljana Grgura Ninskog 3; tel: 021-277 455; daily 8am–midnight; €€

Tucked away in a cosy little square is this equally cosy tavern serving contemporary Dalmatian dishes along with delicious gnocchi stuffed with seafood.

Noštromo
Kraj Svete Marije 10; tel: 091-405 666; daily noon–midnight; €€€

Roast squid and creamy seafood risottos are among the specialities served in a classy modern interior right next to the fish market – guaranteeing freshness.

Central Dalmatia: Trogir

Alka
Augstina Kažotća 15; tel: 021-881 856; www.restaurant-alka.hr; daily lunch and dinner; €€€

This popular fish restaurant serves good-quality seafood on its pleasant stone terrace. Meat-eaters aren't left out, however, as there's a large choice including the succulent Dalmatian *pašticada* beef stew served with gnocchi.

Pizzeria Kristian
Augstina Kažotća 6a; tel: 021-885 172; daily lunch and dinner; €

This small and friendly pizzeria is on a lively square, serving wonderfully thin

Treat yourself to lobster pasta in Hvar

pizzas baked in a wood-fired oven. The pasta is made by hand and is delicious, as are the grilled fish and meat dishes.

Central Dalmatia: Hvar

Antika

Donji Kola 24, Stari Grad; tel: 021-765 479; daily noon–midnight; €€

Local fish, pasta and grilled meats are served in this delightfully quirky little restaurant, with various small terraces and hidden rooms tucked in here and there.

Konoba Menego

Kroz Grodu bb, Hvar Town; tel: 021-717 411; www.menego.hr; daily noon–midnight; €€

Konoba Menego remains a local favourite committed to using all the wonderful products from Hvar. The preparation is traditional, with few fancy touches. Expect smoked meat and cheese, hearty stuffed breads and lots of local olive oil. The restaurant is signposted from the left side of Hvar's main square.

Lucullus

Petra Hektorovića 3, Hvar Town; tel: 098-938 6035; www.lucullous-hvar.com; daily 11am–1am; €€€

This convivial restaurant in the Old town is housed in a restored Venetian palace, and its ornate stone courtyard is the best place to sample top-notch fish dishes and meat grilled in the wood-fired oven.

Restaurant Dalmatino

Sveti Marak 1, Hvar Town; tel: 091-529 3121; daily noon–3pm, 5pm–midnight; €€

Grab a table in the cosy courtyard garden of this friendly steakhouse that also makes an excellent array of fish dishes. If you love steak, you might have a problem narrowing down your choice from the broad selection on offer.

Central Dalmatia: Vis

Konoba Bako

Gundulićeva 1, Komiža; tel: 021-713 742; www.konobabako.hr; daily 4pm–midnight; €€

This family-run casual place overlooks a tiny bay, with tables set by the water's edge. Not surprisingly, deliciously fresh fish is the focus, with simply grilled seafood the perfect accompaniment to the sublime waterside setting.

Pojoda

Don Cvjetika Marasovića 8; tel: 021-711 575; daily lunch and dinner; €€€

This busy yet relaxing fish restaurant has a pleasant courtyard shaded by orange and lemon trees. It can be expensive, especially if you order fish by the weight, but the quality is excellent.

Roki's

Plisko Polje 17; tel: 021-714 004; www.rokis.hr; daily lunch and dinner; €€

This family of winemakers also produces scrumptious food cooked slowly in a *peka,* as well as grilled octopus

Restaurants along Stradun, Dubrovnik's main thoroughfare

and squid – all washed down with their superb wines. It's worth booking ahead, even if you call ahead on the same day.

Bugenvila

Obala Ante Starčevića 9; tel: 020-479 949; daily lunch and dinner; €€

Classic Dalmatian cooking is given a modern touch in this smart harbourside restaurant with friendly service. Seafood-lovers can indulge in butter-poached lobster or monkfish with clams, while carnivores can try the ribeye steak with sweetbreads.

Caffè Bar Zino

Obala Ante Starčevića 9; tel: 020-478 3000; daily 10am–11pm; €

This cheap and cheerful spot by the harbour has a simple menu of pizzas, sandwiches and snacks, but it's immensely good value. The portions are almost embarrassingly huge; you'll need a hearty appetite to finish a pizza on your own. Even the sandwiches are enormous.

Konoba Ivan

Tiha put 5; tel: 020-790 002; daily 10am–11pm; €€

On the other side of the peninsula (but only a few hundred metres if you go across the narrow neck), Konoba Ivan is a small, friendly place right by the water's edge where fresh fish and grilled meat make a good lunch.

Southern Dalmatia: Dubrovnik

360 Restaurant

Svetog Dominika; tel: 020-322 222; www.360dubrovnik.com; Tues–Sun 6.30–11pm; €€€€

A medieval arsenal set in the city walls is the setting for this sophisticated restaurant with fantastic views of the Old Port. They don't skimp on top-class ingredients here: turbot, foie gras and the ubiquitous truffle feature on a Mediterranean menu. Book ahead in high season.

Amfora

Obala Stjepana Radića; tel: 020-419 419; www.amforadubrovnik.com; daily 11am–11pm; €€

It's only a short stroll from Gruž harbour to Amfora, which excels at grilled meats, seafood dishes and pastas. Try to get a table upstairs terrace, if it's open.

Azur

Pobljana 10; tel: 020-324 806; www.azurvision.com; daily noon–11pm; €€

Croatia meets Asia in this laid-back restaurant tucked away near the city walls not far from the Aquarium. The innovative menu is heavy on curry, Japanese and Thai spices livening up chicken, beef and fish dishes served in relaxed surroundings.

Barba

Boškovićeva 5; tel: 091-205 3488; daily 11am–11pm; €

A simple but tasty starter

Between Prijeko and Stradun is this unpretentious little seafood café with a casually rustic interior – just the spot for a quick but delicious lunch. Try the octopus burger or tempura prawns.

Dalmatino

Miha Pracata 6; tel: 091-323 070; wwwldalmatino-dubrovnik.com; daily 11am–7pm; €€

This cosy restaurant in one of the Old Town's narrow streets also features an intimate courtyard. Fresh seafood and meat dishes have clean Mediterranean flavours and include black ink risotto, truffle pasta and seafood skewers.

Dionysus Wine Pub

Za Rokum 5a; tel: 099-649 9244; daily 10am–2am; €

Simple risottos, seafood salads and tapas are served in this small convivial bar that's two streets south of Stradun towards the Pile Gate. Owner Maro is infectious in his enthusiasm for local wines, which are served by the glass.

Gil's Little Bistro

Petrilovrijenci 4; tel: 020-321 168; www.gils.hr; noon–midnight; €€€

Meat-lovers flock to this tiny, lively bistro in a narrow street off Stradun. You choose your cut and it's weighed and priced in front of you to save any nasty surprises at the end of the meal.

Kamenice

Gundulićeva poljana 8; tel: 020-322 682; daily 10am–11pm; €€

Tables spread out in front of this long-established restaurant where fish figures prominently on the menu. It is touristy, certainly, but the grilled squid is particularly good and they also specialise in oysters, after which the restaurant is named. You might want to book ahead.

Lady PiPi

Antuninska 21; tel: 020-321 154; 9am–midnight; €

Don't let the name put you off this appealing place in the shadow of the city walls north of Prijeko. Meat dishes are cooked in front of you on the open barbecue under the vine-covered terrace, and a higher terrace gives you marvellous views of the Old Town. This is a popular place so make sure to get there early.

Lucin Kantun

Od Sigurate; tel: 020-321 003; daily lunch and dinner; €

Just off Stradun is this pleasant, unpretentious place with friendly staff and an open kitchen. The restaurant makes good use of locally grown vegetables and serves some excellent tapas dishes.

Nishta

Prijeko bb; tel: 020-322 088; www.nishtarestaurant.com; Mon–Sat 11.30am–11pm; €

True vegetarian food is hard to come by in Croatia, so it's not surprising that this

Octopus salad is a firm favourite

small restaurant on the corner of Prijeko and Palmotičeva has a devoted following. Asian, Middle Eastern and Mexican flavours mingle with local dishes, and there are vegan and gluten-free options. There's a branch in Zagreb too.

Oyster Bar & Sushi Bota

Od Pustijeme bb; tel: 020-324 034; www.bota-sare.hr; daily 9am–1am; €–€€

Oysters from Ston are given the Japanese treatment in this sleek modern restaurant by the cathedral. In fact, most of the Adriatic fruits of the sea are beautifully turned into sushi, teriyaki and tempura delights. There's also a traditional oyster restaurant in Mali Ston.

Panorama

Upper Cable Car Station, Mount Srđ; tel: 020-312 664; www.dubrovnikcablecar.com; daily lunch and dinner; €€

The views are incomparable in this restaurant at the top of the cable car station. And the food, if a little pricey, is worth the trip up to Mount Srđ either via cable car or the 90-minute hike. It's a good stop for lunch or to catch the sunset.

Pantarul

Kralja Tomislava 1; tel: 020-333 486; www.pantarul.com; daily lunch and dinner; €€

There are a few Asian touches to the mainly Dalmatian menu in this friendly restaurant with a contemporary interior. Well-crafted dishes include slow-roasted pork belly, and the five-course fish and meat tasting menus are very good value. It's worth booking ahead.

Restaurant Kopun

Poljana Ruđera Boškovića 7; tel: 020-323 969; www.restaurantkopun.com; daily lunch and dinner; €€

Fresh seafood and Dalmatian meat dishes are served in this romantic restaurant opposite the Jesuit Church. It's especially atmospheric on warm evenings when the outdoor tables spill into the square.

Rozario

Prijeko 1; tel: 020-322 015; www.konoba-rozario.hr; daily noon–11pm; €€

Romantic Rozario serves up excellent Dalmatian food in a cosy dining room or at a few little tables in a leafy corner outside. Try the seafood stew, which includes shrimp, mussels and fish in a savoury and fragrant broth.

Stara Loza

Prijeko 22; tel: 020-321 145; www.prijekopalace.com; daily noon–11pm; €€€

The restaurant on the ground floor of the Prijeko Palace is as classy as the hotel itself. They do an imaginative take on local cuisine and add a few international dishes to suit all palates. Slow-cooked ox cheeks and the octopus gnocchi with bone marrow are standout dishes.

A rustic setting in Korčula

Taj Mahal

Nikole Gučetića 2; tel: 020-323 221;
www.tajmahal-dubrovnik.com; daily
10am–1.am; €

Get a taste of neighbouring Bosnia in
this cave-like restaurant decorated in
Ottoman style. Dishes include Bosnian
staples such as *ćevapčići* and savoury
burek pastries filled with meat or
cheese. There's another branch at the
Hotel Lero in Lapad.

Southern Dalmatia: Korčula

Adio Mare

Sveti Roka 2; tel: 020-711 253; daily lunch
and dinner; €–€€

Try to get a table on the roof terrace of
this atmospheric restaurant with an
extensive fish and seafood menu including grilled fish and squid. It's worth
booking ahead during high season.

Aterina

Trg Korčulanski Klesara i Kipara 2;
tel: 091-986 1856; daily lunch and dinner;
€–€€

You're at the mercy of the elements in
this genial restaurant, as it is based
purely outside. There are sturdy
umbrellas, however, and luckily the
island is blessed with sunny weather.
As well as seafood and pasta dishes,
you'll feast on lovely tapas which are
good value.

Feral Restoran

Lumbarda; tel: 020-712 090; daily lunch
and dinner; €–€€

Thankfully there's nothing feral about
this chilled-out restaurant by the
water's edge in Lumbarda. Savour
well-priced pasta and seafood dishes
either on the small patio by the water
or the large covered first-floor terrace
with lovely views.

Southern Dalmatia: Mljet

Konoba Galicija

Pomena 7, Pomena; tel: 020-744 029; daily
10am–midnight; €–€€

One of a string of little restaurants along
Pomena's harbourside, Galicija serves
wonderfully fresh seafood and grilled
fish in a simple terrace right beside the
harbour. It's popular among visitors on
sailing holidays as they can moor right
beside the restaurant.

Restoran Stermasi

Saplunara; tel: 098-939 0362;
www.stermasi.hr; daily 10am–midnight;
€–€€

Set on a hillside overlooking the rocky
bay is this enchanting restaurant that
specialises in dishes cooked *ispod
peke* – under a cast-iron bell. These
need to be ordered a couple of hours in
advance, and there's even a vegetarian
version. It's worth the wait.

Aquarius nightclub, Zagreb

NIGHTLIFE

Outdoor nightlife starts in April and reaches a peak in July and August with myriad festivals as well as all-night beach parties. The most fun is to be had on the islands, especially Hvar, where locals seem to have a higher level of noise tolerance, plus the capacity to stay out all night and still function in the morning. For the rest of the year, Zagreb and Split have the most varied nightlife offerings.

In the summer many resorts offer open-air cinema; films are usually shown in their original versions, with Croatian subtitles. The local tourist offices have the schedules.

The clubs, bars and concert venues listed are all accessible from places in the itineraries.

Zagreb

The main centre for bars is in Tkalčićeva in the Upper Town and Bogovićeva in the Lower Town. Just out of town is Lake Jarun, where there is a large choice of clubs, bars and cocktail lounges.

Aquarius
Matije Ljubeka bb; www.aquarius.hr
Zagreb's biggest nightclub is 4km (3 miles) from the centre, overlooking Lake Jarun. It has been a Zagreb institution for many years and is an obligatory stop for night-crawlers of all ages. It also has a very popular outpost on Zrće beach in the island of Pag not far from Split. Dance, commercial and techno predominate on the dance floor. Dress smart.

Bacchus Jazz Bar
Trg kralja Tomislava 16
Quirkily decorated with antiques and less than 100 metres/yds from the train station, this little bar has a cosy garden and live jazz a few nights a week.

Tvornica
Šubićeva 2; www.tvornica.kulture.com
Host to Pixies, Nick Cave, Kurt Vile and David Byrne among others, this exciting venue presents an adventurous programme of concerts, performance art, plays, exhibitions and dazzling shows.

Vastroslav Lisinski Concert Hall
Trg Stjepana Radića 4; www.lisinski.hr
Zagreb has a first-class concert hall to accommodate its culture-loving citizens. Its full schedule of opera, concerts and ballet usually runs from October–May.

Istria: Poreč

Byblos
Zelena Laguna 1; www.byblos.hr
There's a free shuttle to this lively and sprawling club 4km (2.4 miles) south of Poreč, and if you can hang in there till 4am, there's one to take you back.

The bar scene in Split

In the meantime, international DJs play the best in electronic and dance music.

Istria: Pula

Rock Club Uljanik
Dobrilina 2; www.clubuljanik.hr

In a building overlooking the shipyard, this immensely popular club presents live concerts by Croatia's best rockers as well as club nights with DJs. Uljanik is one of the few venues accessible by foot from central Pula.

Central Dalmatia: Split

Bačvice Complex
Bačvice Bay

Ground zero for Split nightlife is the Bačvice complex, 1km (0.75 mile) south of the Old Town. This network of clubs, bars and cafés overlooks Bačvice Beach, Split's public beach.

Ghetto Club
Dosud 10

The young waiters drift pleasantly through the candlelit courtyard, where the music is soft and accompanied by a trickling fountain. From early morning to well past midnight, Ghetto Club provides a relaxing ambience in which to sip drinks and nibble on snacks.

Central Dalmatia: Hvar

Carpe Diem
Riva bb; www.carpe-diem-hvar.com

This cocktail bar has achieved near-legendary status. Almost every celebrity whose yacht docks offshore heads right to the open-air terrace and pricey cocktails of Carpe Diem. During the summer, catch the boat to the Carpe Diem beach on the island of Stipanska for daytime revels as well as full-moon parties.

Southern Dalmatia: Dubrovnik

Banje Beach Restaurant Lounge and Club
Frana Supila; www.ew-dubrovnik.com

The daytime atmosphere in what was the East West club lounge on Banje Beach becomes more sophisticated as the sun goes down and everyone grabs a cocktail. From May–October, it's open till 6am.

Club Lazareti
Frana Supila bb; www.lazareti.com

The 17th-century quarantine barracks near Banje Beach is Dubrovnik's leading cultural and arts venue. It holds everything from folklore performances to underground club nights, mini festivals and outdoor film screenings.

Culture Club Revelin
Ulica Svetog Dominika 3;
www.clubrevelin.com

The imposing fortress hosts club nights with international DJs as well as live bands. Clubbers can take a breather on the giant terrace with views of the Old Town. In July, it attracts top names in electronic music for its annual Revelin Festival, as well as the Du-El Fest electronic music festival in August.

Boat moored in Hvar Town harbour

A–Z

A

Addresses

In Zagreb and Split, street names can be written two ways, in the nominative or possessive case. Occasionally, you will see the letters, 'bb' which stands for *bez broja* (without number). It indicates that there is no numbering on the street. In small towns such as Hvar and Korčula, street names either do not exist or are rarely used. Other than that, the names and numbering of addresses are as you would expect.

C

Children

Croatia has plenty of beaches, which makes the coastline a great place for family vacations. In Istria, Poreč has the widest assortment of family-friendly hotels with a full range of outdoor activities for kids to enjoy. Dubrovnik's Copacabana Beach on the Babin Kuk peninsula has a beach playground, and the shallow waters are safe even for toddlers.

Croatians are generally children-friendly. While few restaurants have high chairs for toddlers, there is a casual dining atmosphere and getting children's meals is rarely a problem. Kids get discounts everywhere – in museums, at hotels and on ferries. The vast array of apartments for rent along the coast can keep costs down for family travel.

Climate

The best time to visit Croatia is during spring and summer, when days are sunny and dry. Coastal temperatures regularly reach 30°C (86°F) in August. The Croatian coast is significantly warmer than its interior. In January, temperatures in the east of the country can fall as low as -1°C (30°F) but can be as high as 10°C (50°F). Expect snow in the interior of the country during the winter, particularly in Zagreb and Plitvice Lakes National Park. In Istria, autumn, although mild, is often wet. Most beaches are pebbly or rocky, and it is advisable to bring swimming shoes – particularly for children. These are easily and cheaply available in beach resorts.

Clothing

Although dress is casual in Croatia, locals tend to be neat dressers, and women pay close attention to fashion trends. Restaurants rarely require a jacket and tie, but it is wise to pack a smart jacket for the more upmarket establishments. Visitors of both sexes should avoid short shorts and bare shoulders while visiting churches. In 2016, Dubrovnik's authorities passed a law fining anyone caught walking in

Exploring Trakošćan Castle

the Old Town dressed only in swimwear. Many young Croatians dress to impress at night; anyone wishing to go to fashionable bars or clubs would be wise to do the same. In spring and autumn, it is best to be prepared for rain and the occasional cooler temperature, but summers are hot, even at night, so you are pretty safe if you pack only lightweight clothing. November to March can be cold, so bring a warm coat.

Crime and Safety

Croatia is relatively safe, but you should take the normal, sensible precautions: be especially careful when withdrawing money from ATMs; hold tight to your belongings in markets and other crowded places; and avoid any insalubrious areas at night, especially if you are alone. In some isolated parts of inland Croatia, particularly in remote parts of Lika and Continental Croatia, there are still some land mines from the 1990s war that have not been cleared yet. Look out for warning signs with the skull and crossbones on a red triangle with black lettering saying *Ne prilazite* (Do not enter), and do not stray from roads and paved areas without a local guide. Avoid overgrown areas and abandoned war-damaged buildings in particular. A useful resource is the Croatian Mine Action group (www.hcr.hr).

Customs

Visitors from other parts of the European Union have no limits on what they can import, as long as they can prove it is for personal use. Visitors from outside the European Union can bring 1 litre of spirits, 2 litres of wine, 200 cigarettes or 50 cigars. If you are carrying more than a total of €10,000 in cash or cheques, you must declare it at customs. Do not be alarmed by random 'everybody off' spot-checks at the border when travelling by train or bus: these searches tend to be for smuggled black-market goods.

Disabled Travellers

The organisation that handles the needs of disabled people in Croatia is Savez Organizacija Invalida Hrvatske (Savska 3, Zagreb 10000; tel: 01-482 9394; www.soih.hr). Many of Croatia's most interesting sights are in historic old towns, where streets are generally cobbled and old buildings have narrow staircases, hallways and no lifts, making disabled access problematic. Access to beaches can also be difficult, although the town of Omiš, near Split, has a wheelchair-accessible beach with special ramps to lower disabled people into the sea. In Dubrovnik, the smooth marble streets of the Old Town make it easy for people in wheelchairs to explore, although people with limited mobility will find it difficult to climb the steps to the higher street and to walk the city walls. However, there is a transporter that can be booked in advance (tel: 098-915 2834).

Hvar Town café

Many large hotels are wheelchair-accessible, and usually public toilets in major cities are too. Public buses and trams are usually not wheelchair-accessible. Most local ferries have lifts. See www.jadrolinija.hr for more details on wheelchair-accessible ferries.

E

Electricity

The electrical current is 220 volts ac, 50Hz. Most sockets have two round pins. UK visitors should pack an adaptor (available from airports, chemists' stores, supermarkets, etc.) for appliances brought from home. US and Canadian visitors will need a transformer for 110-volt appliances.

Embassies and Consulates

Embassies and consulates in Croatia
Australia: Centar Kaptol, Nova Ves II; tel: 01-489 1200.
Canada: Prilaz Đure Deželića 4, Zagreb; tel: 01-488 1200.
New Zealand: Vlaška ulica 50a, Zagreb; tel: 01-461 2060.
UK: Ivana Lučića 4, Zagreb; tel: 01-600 9100; Obala hrvatskog narodnog preporoda 10/III, Split; tel: 021-341 464.
US: Thomasa Jeffersona 2, Zagreb; tel: 01-661 2200.

Croatian embassies and consulates
Australia:14 Jindalee Cres, O'Malley, Canberra; tel: 02-6286 6988.

Canada: 229 Chapel St, Ottawa; tel: 613-562 7820.
New Zealand: 131 Lincoln Road, Henderson, Auckland; tel: 09-836 5581.
South Africa: 1160 Church St, 0083 Colbyn, Pretoria; tel: 012-342 1206.
UK: 21 Conway St, London; tel: 020-7387 2022.
US: 2343 Massachusetts Ave NW, Washington, DC; tel: 202-588 5899; www.croatiaemb.org.

Emergencies

Police: 192
Fire brigade: 193
Ambulance: 194
Road assistance: 1987

Etiquette

Croatians tend to be quite reserved with strangers, especially away from the main tourist areas. A few words of Croatian go a long way. When addressing strangers it is polite to use the honorific *gospodine* (for a man), *gospođo* (for a married woman) or *gospodice* (for a young unmarried woman), followed by the family name. Beachwear is not acceptable in churches and visitors should cover their shoulders and knees. As a visit to any café will quickly confirm, Croatians take their fashion seriously and do not appreciate scruffy dress. If invited to a Croatian house for a meal, it is appropriate to give the hostess an odd number of flowers, from three upwards (but not chrysanthemums, which symbolise death), and the host a bottle of

Patriotic flip flops

good wine or a box of chocolates. Do not start eating before the host. Croatians hold the fork in the left hand and the knife in the right. It is polite to wait for the host to insist before accepting a second helping. It is advisable to exercise tact when discussing politics or history.

Gay and Lesbian Travellers

Homosexuality is legal in Croatia but not fully accepted. As a result, there are not many officially gay venues. Discos and bars in major cities such as Zagreb and Dubrovnik are usually gay-friendly, but public displays of affection are frowned upon. On the last Saturday in June, Croatia's LGBT population comes out of the closet and flocks to Zagreb's Gay Pride Day. The rest of the year, gays head to naturist beaches to meet others, but note that these are not exclusively gay beaches.

H

Health

No vaccinations are required to enter Croatia and there are no particular health issues in the country. Tap water is safe to drink everywhere.

Medical services

There are reciprocal healthcare agreements between most EU countries and Croatia, entitling such citizens to free medical care, although payment is required for prescribed medicines. UK nationals should carry a European Health Insurance card (EHIC), which entitles them to state-provided medical treatment. However, in order to cover all eventualities (including repatriation), it is advisable to take out private travel insurance before leaving home.

If your country does not have an agreement with Croatia, you will have to pay according to listed prices. Most doctors speak some English. In an emergency, go to *hitna pomoć* (casualty).

Pharmacies

Pharmacies are open Monday–Friday 8am–7pm, Saturday 8am–2pm. The following are open 24 hours:
Zagreb: Ilica 43, tel: 01-484 8450.
Split: Dobri, Gundulićeva 52; tel: 021-348 074; and Lučas, Pupačićeva 4; tel: 021-533 188.
Dubrovnik: Two pharmacies alternate weekly. In the Old Town, Ljekarna Kod Zvonika, Placa; tel: 020-321 133; and, near Gruž harbour, Ljekarna Gruž, Gruška obala; tel: 020-418 990.

Holidays

Banks, post offices and most shops close on public holidays.
1 Jan: New Year's Day
6 Jan: Epiphany
Late Mar or early/mid-Apr: Easter Sunday and Monday
1 May: May Day
60 days after Easter: Corpus Christi (May/June)

Croatian newspapers

22 June: Anti-Fascist Struggle Day
25 June: Croatian National Day
5 Aug: National Thanksgiving Day
15 Aug: Feast of the Assumption
8 Oct: Independence Day
1 Nov: All Saints' Day
25 and 26 Dec: Christmas

Hours

Banks. Most banks are open Monday–Friday 8am–4pm, and some open on Saturday 7am–1pm.

Churches. These are generally open 8am–noon and 4–7.30pm, although some stay open all day from July to August, while others have more irregular hours. Remote churches open only for their respective saint's days.

Food shops. Most food shops are open Monday–Friday 7am–8pm, Saturday 7am–1pm. The majority of towns have at least one food store open on Sunday morning, but a recent law mandating Sunday closings may mean that this is not to be counted on. Food markets are usually open only in the morning.

Museums. Most museums open 9am–noon; in summer many stay open in the afternoon, and in the resorts some open in the evening in peak season. Dubrovnik's museums generally open 9am–6pm in summer. Some museums close on Sunday, others on Monday.

Local tourist offices. Local tourist offices have three seasons: winter, shoulder and summer season. In the winter, hours are regular business hours, that is Monday to Friday from 8 or 9am to noon or 1pm and then from about 2–5pm. In the shoulder season (May, June, September) hours are extended to Saturday morning. In July and August hours are long, often from 8am to 8pm daily.

Post offices. Most post offices are open Monday–Friday 7.30am–7pm, Saturday 8am–1pm.

Shops. Along the coast, clothes shops, bookshops, museums and the like close for a long lunchtime siesta. Their opening times are roughly Monday–Saturday 8am–1pm and 4–7pm. In major tourist areas, some shops open from 8am–8pm.

Maps

City bookshops sell road maps. The tourist board publishes an excellent free map, and many local tourist offices provide useful, detailed town maps. Also handy are the Insight Fleximaps to the Croatian Coast and Dubrovnik, laminated for durability and easy folding.

Media

Newspapers. In summer, foreign newspapers and magazines are available in all the main resorts. Online English-language newspapers include *The Dubrovnik Times* (www.thedubrovniktimes.com), which covers the city specifically, and *Croatia Week* (www.croatiaweek.com).

Police car in Zagreb

Radio. Hrvatska Radio (www.radio.hrt.hr) broadcasts news and magazine programmes nationally, and also has regional stations in Dubrovnik, Knin, Osijek, Pula, Rijeka, Sljeme, Split and Zadar. All are available online. During the summer season, it broadcasts traffic and sailing reports in English, German and Italian. The corporation also produces Glas Hrvatske (Voice of Croatia; www.glashrvatske.hrt.hr), which has programmes in English, German and Spanish.

Television. Hrvastka radiotelevizija (HRT; www.hrt.hr) has four terrestrial public television channels (HRT1–HRT4). The majority of foreign-language programmes, of which there are many, are shown in their original language with Croatian subtitles.

Money

Cash machines. Banks in large towns and resorts have ATMs. Look for the *bancomat* sign.

Credit cards. Most hotels, restaurants and shops accept major credit cards. Small *konobe* in out-of-the-way villages are not usually equipped to accept credit cards, and if you stay in private accommodation, you must pay in cash. It's always worth checking in advance.

Currency. The Croatian kuna (officially abbreviated as HRT, but most commonly written as Kn) is divided into 100 lipa. Foreign currency can be imported and exported freely. Any-

thing up to 15,000Kn can be exported. The exchange rate is fixed and varies by season. Although the euro is not official currency, hotel room prices are often quoted in euros. Many businesses will accept euros but will give change in kuna.

Traveller's cheques. The only reliable place to cash traveller's cheques is at an authorised change place, *Mjenačnica*. The exchange rate on traveller's cheques is generally not as favourable as the rate on cash or what you get withdrawing from a cash machine.

Police

Croatian police wear dark-blue uniforms and are generally helpful and friendly; many speak some English.

Anyone involved in a road traffic accident is legally required to report it to the police. In an emergency, dial 192 or 112.

Postal Services

The Croatian postal service (www.posta.hr) handles mail quickly and efficiently. Stamps for international mail must be purchased at post offices, which are open from 7.30am to 7pm weekdays and from 8am to 1pm on Saturday. In addition to selling stamps, post offices sell SIM cards and prepaid cards. Do not expect post office personnel to speak much English.

Sundial in Hvar Town

S

Smoking

Smoking is banned in all enclosed public places, including bars, restaurants and cafés. However, be prepared for plenty of smoke wafting around outdoor terraces in cafés and restaurants. As in other parts of Europe, e-cigarettes are growing in popularity.

T

Telephones

To call Croatia from abroad, dial 385.

Direct international calls can be made from blue public phone booths on the street with a phone card available from newspaper kiosks. Or you can call from an HTP cabin (Croatian Telecoms), and pay when you have finished. Calls are cheaper between 7pm and 6am.

Dial 00 to call abroad, followed by the country code (UK: 44; Canada and US: 1; Australia: 61), then the number you wish to reach, omitting any initial zero.
International operator: 901
International directory inquiries: 902
Local directory inquiries: 988
Mobile phones. Croatia is on the GSM 900/1800 frequency, which means that American mobile (cell) phones that aren't quad band and still run on the GSM 850/1900 frequency are not compatible. Call charges are the same as in other European Union countries.

A SIM card costs from 10Kn. You can buy a mobile or SIM card at some post offices or the shops of Croatia's main providers: T-Mobile, Vipnet and Tele2. Be aware that, in some inland regions, 3G coverage can be patchy.

In Croatia, numbers that begin with 09 are mobile phones and are billed at a higher rate.

Time Differences

Croatia is one hour ahead of gmt: if it is noon in London, it is 1pm in Zagreb. Daylight saving is used.

Tipping

Restaurant bills usually include service. However, it is common practice to round up the bill to the nearest 10 kuna or leave an extra 10 per cent if the service has been good. In cheaper restaurants, it is normal to leave any coins from the change. Unless the service has been exceptional, do not feel obliged to tip taxi drivers as they often overcharge tourists or round up the fare.

Toilets

Croatia has standard Western toilets. Public toilets often require payment of 2Kn to the toilet attendant.

Tourist Information

The Croatian National Tourist Board and all the local tourist boards publish reams of information and maps that can be invaluable in planning your trip.

Art for sale in Poreč

Tourist information offices

Croatian National Tourist Board (Zagreb): Ilberov Trg 10/4, Zagreb; tel: 01-469 9333; www.croatia.hr.

Zagreb City: Trg Bana Jelačića 11, Zagreb; tel: 01-481 4051; www.infozagreb.hr.

Plitvice Lakes National Park: Plitvička jezera; tel: 053-751 015; www.np-plitvicka-jezera.hr.

Istria County: Pionirska 1, Poreč; tel: 052-452 797; www.istra.hr.

Pula: Forum 3; tel: 052-219 197; www.pulainfo.com.

Poreč: Zagrebačka 9, Poreč; tel: 052-451 293; www.to-porec.hr.

Rovinj: Obala Pina Budicina, Rovinj; tel: 052-811 566; www.tzgrovinj.hr.

Pazin: Franine i Jurine 14, Pazin; tel: 052-622 460; www.central-istria.com.

Motovun: Trg Andrea Antico 1, Motovun; tel: 052-681 726; www.tz-motovun.hr.

Grožnjan: Ulica Gorjan 3, Grožnjan; tel: 052-776 349; www.tz-groznjan.hr.

Split: Peristil bb; tel: 021-342 606; www.visitsplit.com.

Trogir: Trg Ivana Pavla II 1, Trogir; tel: 021-885 628; www.tztrogir.hr.

Makarska: Obala kralja Tomislava, 16 Makarska; tel: 021-612 002; www.makarska-info.hr.

Krka National Park: Trg Ivana Pavla II 5, Šibenik; tel: 022-210 777; www.npkrka.hr.

Šibenik: Obala Franje Tuđmana, Šibenik; tel: 022-214 411; www.sibenik-tourism.hr.

Vis: Šetalište Stare Isse 5, Vis; tel: 021-717 017; www.tz-vis.hr.

Komiža: Riva sv. Mikule 2, Komiža; tel: 021-713 455; www.tz-komiza.hr.

Hvar: Trg sv. Stjepana 42, Hvar; tel: 021-741 059; www.tzhvar.hr.

Dubrovnik: Brsalje 5, tel: 021-323 887; www.tzdubrovnik.hr.

Mljet: Zabrježe 2, Babino Polje; tel 020-746 025; www.mljet.hr; National Park: Polače; tel: 020-744 041; www.np-mljet.hr.

Tourist offices abroad

UK: Third Floor, No. 1 Farrier's Yard, 77–85 Fulham Palace Road, London W6 9ER; tel: 020-8563 7979; www.croatia.hr.

US: 350 Fifth Avenue, Suite 4003, New York 10118; tel: 212-279 8672.

Croatian Angels

This is a service that has been set up to assist visitors. For general tourist information, between 1 April and 31 October, tel: 062-999 999 (+385-62-999 999 if calling from abroad). The service is available in English, Italian, German and Croatian.

Transport

Arrival by air

Croatia's national airline, **Croatia Airlines** (www.croatiaairlines.com), operates direct scheduled flights from London to Zagreb and Dubrovnik. Flying time from London is just over two hours. In summer, the timetable is extended to include flights to Split and Rijeka. The company also operates flights from

On the road to Dubrovnik

most other principal European cities, but has no direct routes from the US.

British Airways (www.britishairways. com) flies from London to Zagreb and Dubrovnik. Budget airlines include **easy-Jet** (www.easyjet.com) from London to Split, Pula and Dubrovnik; **Ryanair** (www. ryanair.com) from London to Rijeka, Zadar and Osijek; **Wizzair** (wizzair.com) from London to Split, and Flybe (www. flybe.com) from Birmingham, Manchester, Edinburgh and Newcastle to Zagreb.

The following airlines also fly to Croatia: Air France, Air Serbia, Alitalia, Aeroflot, Austrian Airlines, Brussels Airlines, ČSA Czech Airlines, FlyDubai, Germanwings, Lufthansa, Norwegian, Swiss, TAP Portugal, Turkish Airlines, Vueling and Qatar Airways.

From April to September, it is possible to find charter flights. These normally fly to Split, Dubrovnik and Pula.

To and from the airport

Croatia Airlines runs a bus service to and from Zagreb airport to Zagreb Centre, with departures every 30 minutes. In Split and Dubrovnik, airport buses leave 90 minutes prior to the plane's take off, while buses from the airport leave shortly after the planes arrive. For further information about airport bus links, contact: Zagreb (tel: 01-633 1999), Split (tel: 021-203 119), Dubrovnik (tel: 060-305 070).

Arrival by road

To enter Croatia by car you require a green insurance card, which should be supplied by your rental company if you are hiring a car. The main road into the country from Western Europe is the E70, bringing you from Trieste, Italy, to pass through Slovenia for border crossings south for Istria and Dalmatia, or east for Zagreb.

Arrival by train

There are train services direct to Zagreb from Italy, Slovenia, Austria, Hungary, Serbia, Bosnia-Herzegovina, France, Germany and Switzerland. The daily EuroCity 'Mimara' service runs from Munich, through Austria, to arrive in Zagreb via Ljubljana. Intercity trains run from Venice, Trieste, Vienna, Budapest and Belgrade.

For details of travelling from London to Croatia by train, see www.seat61.com.

Arrival by sea

You can get to Dalmatia by ferry from Italy. Year round, **Jadrolinija** (tel: +385-51-666 111; www.jadrolinija.hr), the Croatian national ferry company, runs regular services from Ancona to Split, Hvar and Zadar, and from Bari to Dubrovnik. Another Croatian company (but with a helpline based in Malta), **Blue Line** (tel: +356 2122 3299; www. blueline-ferries.com), also covers the Ancona−Split route and runs summer ferries from Ancona to Hvar.

To travel to Istria from Italy in the summer, take Venezia Lines (tel: +352-52-422 896; www.venezialines.com) from Venice to Pula, Rovinj, Poreč or Umag.

Coastal ferry operator

Getting around

Bus. A comprehensive coach network connects all parts of the country and is extremely reliable. Coaches can get busy in summer, though, so it is wise to pick up your ticket in advance at the bus station. Tickets cannot be purchased online. For times, contact Zagreb main bus station (tel: 060-313 333 or +385-1-611 2789 outside Croatia; www.akz.hr).

Taxi. Taxis are available in all major towns and resorts. Drivers are obliged to run a meter.

Driving. The Adriatic Highway coastal road (*Jadranska magistrala*) is full of twists and turns, but the views are amazing. It is very well maintained but can be extremely slow going in the height of summer as there is only one lane each way. There is also a two-lane motorway that runs parallel to just north of the Pelješac peninsula and is considerably further inland. It won't be as scenic, but it will save you hours. When driving down the coast towards Dubrovnik, bear in mind that the road crosses in and out of Bosnia. Have your passports ready to be inspected, and also be prepared for very long queues at the border during high season.

The police are quick to catch speeding motorists, which can result in on-the-spot fines. The speed limit in towns is 50kmh (30mph); out of town it is 80kmh (50mph); and on motorways 130kmh (80mph). For cars towing caravans or trailers it is 80kmh (50mph). The blood alcohol limit is 0.5 per cent.

Driving under the influence can lead to severe fines and the confiscation of your licence. Tolls are payable on a number of motorways, and for passage through the Učka Tunnel between Rijeka and Istria.

Finding parking spaces in the coastal towns can be difficult, especially during peak season, as all central parking spots are reserved for residents with permits. If you abuse local parking restrictions, you risk having your vehicle towed away.

Another disadvantage of travelling by car arises when it comes to 'island hopping'. Vehicles frequently have to queue for hours before boarding ferries. Taking a car on a ferry can also be expensive; it may be cheaper and easier to rent a car once you reach the island and can decide if you need it. Also be warned that, if you are driving during the winter months, especially in the mountains, winter tyres are essential, and in extreme cases snow chains have to be used. Drivers must have their lights switched on when there is poor visibility and also all day during the winter – from the last Sunday in October to the last Sunday in March – or risk getting fined.

Hrvatski Autoklub (Croatian Automobile Club) provides a 24-hour breakdown service (tel: 987; www.hak.hr).

Car rental. There are services in all main towns, tourist resorts and airports. In addition to local car-rental companies, global companies such as Avis, Budget and Hertz are well represented. Web portals such as Economy Car Rent-

als (www.economycarrentals.com) and carrentals.co.uk can offer some very good deals.

Drivers must be over 21 years old and have held a valid driving licence for a minimum of two years. A credit card and a current passport or national identity card are also required for car hire.

Motorbike. The coastal road from Istria down to south Dalmatia makes a fantastic trip for bikers. What's more, with a motorbike you can reach the more remote villages on the islands, without having the trauma that car drivers experience of waiting for hours to board ferries. (Bikes tend to queue-jump and are waved straight on.)

Ferry. Jadrolinija is the main operator for the dozens of local ferries that connect the island with the coastal ports of Dubrovnik, Makarska, Split, Zadar and Rijeka. The winter schedule runs from October to May; the summer schedule from June to September. Services are more frequent and more expensive in the summer.

There is also a private company, **MB Kapetan Luka TP** (tel: 021-645 476; www.krilo.hr), that runs a passenger boat connecting Split, Hvar and Korčula all year, and another, **G&V** (tel: 060-100 000; www.gv-line.hr) that connects Dubrovnik with Polače (Mljet Island), the Elaphiti islands and Korčula (summer only).

Train. Rail travel is limited, but **Hrvatske Željeznice** (Croatian Railways; tel: 060-333 444; www.hznet.hr) runs a slow, comfortable overnight service, with sleeper compartments, between Zagreb and Split via Zadar and Šibenik. A quicker way to reach the coast is to take one of the two high-speed trains that connect Zagreb to Split in 5.5 hours. There is no rail line to Dubrovnik. A good daytime service runs between Zagreb and Rijeka, passing through the beautiful forests of Gorski Kotar.

Travel companies

UK companies offering package holidays to Croatia include:

Activities Abroad: tel: +44 (0)1670 789991; www.activities.abroad. Specialist provider of activity holidays focusing on families.

Adriatic Holidays: tel: +44 (0)1865 339481; www.adriaticholidaysonline.com. Specialises in sailing holidays along the Dalmatian coast. Offers organised trips and charters.

Anatolian Sky: tel: +44 (0)12 764 3553; www.anatoliansky.co.uk.

Balkan Escape: tel: +44 (0)1775 719891; www.balkanescape.co.uk.

Balkan Holidays: tel: +44 (0)20 7543 5555; www.balkanholidays.co.uk.

Completely Croatia: tel: +44 (0)1323 832538; www.completelycroatia.co.uk.

Chalfont Holidays: tel: +44 (0)1753 740176; www.chalfontholidays.co.uk. Specialist providers of naturist holidays in Croatia.

Exodus: tel: +44 (0)20 3811 3949; www.exodus.co.uk. Activity holidays including cycling in Istria, Dalmatia and

Autumn colours in Plitvice National Park

Plitvice Lakes.

Flexitreks tel: +44 (0)1273 410550; www.flexitrek.com. Cycling holidays in Croatia all along the Adriatic coast, with some holidays combining sailing and biking.

Original Travel: tel: (0)20 3603 6518; www.originaltravel.co.uk. Luxury holidays in boutique hotels in Dalmatia and Istria.

Prestige Holidays: tel: +44 (0)1425 480400; www.prestigeholidays.co.uk. Luxury holiday specialists with an extensive collection of Croatian destinations

Regent Holidays: tel: +44 (0)20 3733 5024; www.regent-holidays.co.uk.

Thomson Holidays: tel: +44 (0)871 231 4691; www.thomson.co.uk.

UTracks: tel: +44 (0)845 241 7599; www.utracks.com. Specialists in cycling and activity holidays.

Vintage Travel: tel: +44 (0)1954 261 431; www.vintage-travel.co.uk. Offers villa rentals in Istria and in and around Dubrovnik.

Croatian tour companies: travel agents in Croatia offer a variety of specialist tours, activities or holidays including cruising, climbing, sailing, water sports, hunting, fishing, diving, adventure holidays, horse riding, mountain biking, coach tours and wine tours. The two biggest travel agents are Atlas and Generalturist; they both have branches across the country:

Atlas: tel: 01 245 1611; www.atlas-croatia.com;

Generalturist: tel: 01 480 5688; www.general-turist.com.

Other specialist operators include:

Active Holidays Croatia: Knezova kaccića, Omiš; tel: 021-861 829; www.activeholidays-croatia.com. Offers active and sailing holidays all along the Adriatic coast.

Wear Active: Gornji Rukovac, Vis; tel: 021-714 040; www.wearactive.com. Small British company offering kayaking and other activities in Vis.

Visas and Passports

EU passport-holders and US, Canadian, Australian and New Zealand nationals do not need visas and can stay for up to three months. However, because Croatian visitors need a visa to enter the US, the European Commission is considering whether to impose visas for US citizens visiting Croatia because of a lack of visa reciprocity. American citizens should check with their embassy before they travel.

Websites

Visit the tourist office site (www. croatia.hr) for an overview; Croatia Traveller (www.croatiatraveller.com) for travel planning; and the Croatian Homepage (www.hr) for useful links. For private accommodation, try www.adriatica.net, www.adriagate.net and www.atlas-croatia.com, which also organises excursions and ferry bookings.

Street sign

LANGUAGE

Croatian is a difficult language to grasp; it's an inflected language with seven cases and complicated grammar. Although most people in the tourism industry speak English well, a few words of Croatian are appreciated in rural regions.

Croatian football shirts

Wine (white, red, rosé) *vino (bijelo, crno, roze)*
Bread *kruh*
Cheese *sir*
Cold meat *hladno pečenje*
Ham (raw, cooked, smoked) *šunka (sirova, kuhana, dimljena)*
Olives *masline*
Soup *juha*
Beefsteak *biftek*
Chicken *pile*
Pork chops *svinjski kotleti*
Lamb on the spit *janje na ražnju*
Turkey *tuka*
Veal cutlet *teleći odrezak*
Green pepper *paprika*
Mushrooms *gljive*
Onion *luk*
Potato *krumpir*
Salad *salata*
Cake *kolač*
Ice cream *sladoled*
Pancakes *palačinke*

Numbers

0 *nula*
1 *jedan*
2 *dva*
3 *tri*
4 *četiri*
5 *pet*
6 *šest*
7 *sedam*
8 *osam*
9 *devet*
10 *deset*
100 *sto*
1,000 *tisuću*

Shopping

Do you have …? *Imate li …?*
How much is it …? *Kolika košta …?*
Bakery *pekara*
Butchers *mesnica*
Grocer *dućan*
Market *tržnica*
Pastry shop *slastičarnica*
Supermarket *samoposluživanje*
Price *cijena*
Cheap *jeftino*
Expensive *skupo*

Getting around

Where is the …? *Gdje je …?*
railway station? *željeznička postaja?*
bus stop? *autobusna postaja?*
What time does the … leave? *U koliko sati polazi …?*
train/bus/ferry? *vlak/autobus/trajekt?*
one way/return ticket *jednosmjerna/ povratna karta*
Booking *rezervacija*
Timetable *raspored*
How much is the ticket to …? *Koliko košta karta za …?*

Social media

Are you on Facebook/Twitter? *Jesi li na Facebooku/Twitteru?*
What's your username? *Koje ti je korisničko ime?*
I'll add you as a friend. *Dodat ću te za prijatelja.*
I'll follow you on Twitter. *Slijedit ću te na Twitteru.*
I'll put the pictures on Facebook/Twitter. *Stavit ću slike na Facebook/Twitter.*

Reading on the ferry

BOOKS AND FILM

Croatia's complex and turbulent past has been explored, examined and pondered over by many writers over the centuries – some native to the country and others who discovered it on their travels and found it hard to leave. Contemporary Croatian writers such as Slavenka Drakulić and Dubravka Ugrešić excel at turning their experiences of growing up under communism and then enduring the horrors of the 1990s wars into viscerally perceptive and often blackly comic novels.

In cinema, Croatia is a popular setting for Western films thanks to a vibrant film industry and highly regarded local production companies. Over the past 15 years, the country's film-makers have entered a new golden age after the industry's collapse in the 1990s, as its films win more plaudits at international film festivals.

Books

History

The National Question in Yugoslavia by Ivo Banac. An examination of the tension between Serbian nationalism, Croatian nationalism and Yugoslavianism in the Balkans from the mid-19th century to the 1921 Vidovdan Constitution.

The Balkans 1804–1999: Nationalism, War and the Great Powers by Misha Glenny. An ambitious attempt to explain the history of the Balkans and how the rest of the world meddled in its affairs.

The Impossible Country: A Journey Through the Last Days of Yugoslavia by Brian Hall. This engrossing account of the author's journey during the last days of Yugoslavia in 1991 reveals how everyday citizens can be persuaded to think the worst of their neighbours just because they happen to come from a different ethnic background.

The Death of Yugoslavia by Laura Silber and Allan Little. A riveting account of the events that contributed to the 1991 war and running on to the Dayton Accord, presented from a historical perspective.

Croatia: A Nation Forged in War by Marcus Tanner. This is a compelling account of Croatian history that ranges from the Greeks and Romans to the present day.

The Demise of Yugoslavia: A Political Memoir by Stjepan Mesić. This insightful account of the collapse of Yugoslavia was written by the federation's last president, and the first democratically elected president of the independent Croatian state.

The Yugoslav Auschwitz and the Vatican: The Croatian Massacre of the Serbs During World War II by Vladimir Dedijer. Written by a former Yugoslav ambassador to the UN, this impeccably researched book covers a secret episode of the 20th century and one that many Croatians – and Roman Catholics – would prefer had remained secret.

How We Survived Communism and Even Laughed by Slavenka Drakulić. A col-

'Game of Thrones' is partly filmed in Dubrovnik

lection of essays that examine different aspects of life under Communism, including censorship and consumerism.

Balkan Express by Slavenka Drakulić. A fascinating insight, given through a series of essays, into the effects of the Homeland War on the lives of ordinary people.

Croatia Through History by Branka Magaš. Croatian historian and journalist Branka Magaš bravely attempts to cover objectively the history of Croatia from the Middle Ages to the present and does it remarkably well.

Gastronomy

A Taste of Croatia: Savoring the Food, People and Traditions of Croatia's Adriatic Coast by Karen Evenden. Not so much a cookbook as a well-written and lengthy love letter celebrating its subject.

My Favourite Croatian Recipes by Sandra Lougher. One of very few books about Croatian food in English, this includes more than 60 recipes from all over the country.

The Best of Croatian Cooking – Expanded Edition by Liliana Pavičić and Gordana Pirker-Mosher. As well as 200 recipes, the book has an introduction covering Croatia's culinary tradition and a useful wine guide.

Travel

Croatia: Travels in Undiscovered Country by Tony Fabijančić. A travelogue written a Canadian-born son of Croatian immigrants who decided to explore the back roads of his ancestral homeland.

Black Lamb and Grey Falcon by Rebecca West. West's colossal and seminal account of several journeys through Yugoslavia during the 1930s remains essential reading to anyone who wants a deeper understanding of Balkan history.

Fiction

The Museum of Unconditional Surrender by Dubravka Ugrešić. A well-written novel that weaves humour and bitterness. This prize-winning novelist hones in on the life of a 45-year-old Croatian woman living in exile.

Croatian Nights ed. Borivoj Radaković, Matt Thorne and Tony White. An eclectic but brilliant collection of short stories by Croatian and British writers, which grew out of a movement called FAK – Festival of Alternative Literature. It gives an insight into how young writers look at the country.

Television and film

Game of Thrones. Several series of HBO's incredibly popular fantasy drama set in the Middle Ages have been filmed in Dubrovnik, as the city's landmarks stood in admirably well for the fictional King's Landing.

Cure: The Life of Another (2014). Dubrovnik just after the 1991–92 siege is the setting for this unsettling thriller about two teenage girls.

Penelope (2009). Filmed in Dubrovnik, this Croatian-Australian co-production takes the woman's point of view in Homer's Odyssey, as long-suffering Penelope waits for her husband Odysseus to return.

ABOUT THIS BOOK

This *Explore Guide* has been produced by the editors of Insight Guides, whose books have set the standard for visual travel guides since 1970. With top-quality photography and authoritative recommendations, these guidebooks bring you the very best routes and itineraries in the world's most exciting destinations.

INTRODUCTION

The routes are set in context by this introductory section, giving an overview of the destination to set the scene, plus background information on food and drink, shopping and more, while a succinct history timeline highlights the key events over the centuries.

BEST ROUTES

The routes in the book provide something to suit all budgets, tastes and trip lengths. As well as covering the destination's many classic attractions, the itineraries track lesser-known sights. The routes embrace a range of interests, so whether you are an art fan, a gourmet, a history buff or have kids to entertain, you will find an option to suit.

We recommend reading the whole of a route before setting out. This should help you to familiarise yourself with it and enable you to plan where to stop for refreshments – options are shown in the 'Food and Drink' box at the end of each tour.

For our pick of the tours by theme, consult Recommended Routes for… (see pages 6–7).

DIRECTORY

Also supporting the routes is a Directory chapter, with a clearly organised A–Z of practical information, our pick of where to stay while you are there and select restaurant listings; these eateries complement the more low-key cafés and restaurants that feature within the routes and are intended to offer a wider choice for evening dining. Also included here are some nightlife listings, plus a handy language guide and our recommendations for books and films about the destination.

ABOUT THE AUTHORS

Mary Novakovich is an award-winning journalist and travel writer based in Hertfordshire. She has been visiting Croatia, where her parents were born, since the 1970s and goes back whenever humanly possible. When she's not updating guidebooks, she contributes regularly to British newspapers including *The Independent* and *The Guardian*.

CONTACT THE EDITORS

We hope you find this Explore Guide useful, interesting and a pleasure to read. If you have any questions or feedback on the text, pictures or maps, please do let us know. If you have noticed any errors or outdated facts, or have suggestions for places to include on the routes, we would be delighted to hear from you. Please drop us an email at hello@insightguides.com. Thanks!

CREDITS

Explore Croatia
Editor: Carine Tracanelli
Author: Mary Novakovich
Head of Production: Rebeka Davies
Picture Editor: Tom Smyth
Cartography: original cartography Berndtson & Berndtson GmbH, updated by Carte
Photo credits: Alamy 73L, 137; Boutique Pine Tree Resort 108; Carlson Rezidor Hotel Group 109; Corrie Wingate/Apa Publications 4ML, 4MC, 4MR, 4MR, 4MC, 4ML, 6TL, 6BC, 7T, 7M, 8MC, 8ML, 8MC, 8MR, 11B, 12T, 13L, 12B, 12/13, 14B, 15, 16, 17L, 16/17, 18, 19L, 18/19, 22, 23L, 24, 26ML, 26MC, 26MR, 26ML, 26MC, 26MR, 28, 29L, 30, 31L, 30/31, 32, 33L, 34, 35L, 34/35, 36, 37, 38B, 39L, 38/39, 40, 41, 42, 42/43, 44, 46, 46/47, 47L, 48, 49L, 50, 51, 52, 53L, 52/53, 56, 57, 58, 59L, 58/59, 60, 60/61, 61L, 65L, 64/65, 70, 71, 72, 72/73, 75, 76, 77L, 76/77, 78, 79L, 78/79, 95, 97L, 96/97, 103, 111, 114, 115, 117, 118, 120, 121, 122, 123, 124, 125, 126, 127, 128, 129, 131, 132, 133, 134, 135, 136; Dominic Burdon/APA Publications 7MR, 8ML, 8MR, 10, 11T, 14T, 28/29, 32/33, 38T, 43L, 45, 48/49, 54, 55, 62, 63, 64, 66/67, 68, 68/69, 69L, 83L, 82/83, 90/91, 93, 94, 96, 110, 112, 113, 116, 119; Esplanade Zagreb Hotel 98ML, 98MC, 98MR, 98MR, 98MC, 98ML, 101; Getty Images 1, 4/5T, 8/9T, 20, 26/27T, 74, 80/81, 86, 88/89, 98/99T; Goran Ergović/Croatian National Tourist Board 6MC; Hilton Worldwide 100; iStock 6ML, 25, 82, 85, 87, 90, 91L, 130; Leonardo 102, 105, 107; Mario Romulić & Dražen Stojčić/Croatian National Tourist Board 22/23; Photoshot 84; Riva Hvar Yacht Harbor Hotel 106; Shutterstock 7MR, 21, 92; Starwood Hotels & Resorts 104
Cover credits: Shutterstock (main) iStock (bottom)
Printed by CTPS – China
All Rights Reserved
© 2017 Apa Digital (CH) AG and Apa Publications (UK) Ltd

First Edition 2017

DISTRIBUTION

UK, Ireland and Europe
Apa Publications (UK) Ltd
sales@insightguides.com
United States and Canada
Ingram Publisher Services
ips@ingramcontent.com
Australia and New Zealand
Woodslane
info@woodslane.com.au
Southeast Asia
Apa Publications (Singapore) Pte
singaporeoffice@insightguides.com
Hong Kong, Taiwan and China
Apa Publications (HK) Ltd
hongkongoffice@insightguides.com
Worldwide
Apa Publications (UK) Ltd
sales@insightguides.com

SPECIAL SALES, CONTENT LICENSING AND COPUBLISHING

Insight Guides can be purchased in bulk quantities at discounted prices. We can create special editions, personalised jackets and corporate imprints tailored to your needs.
sales@insightguides.com
www.insightguides.biz

INDEX

MAP LEGEND

●	Start of tour	═══ Railway	† Monastery
→	Tour & route direction	═══ Motorway	✡ Synagogue
❶	Recommended sight	·─·─ Ferry route	▬ ─ ▬ National boundary
❷	Recommended restaurant/café	🚌 Main bus station	Important building
★	Place of interest	✈ Airport	Hotel
❶	Tourist information	⚑ Lighthouse	Shopping /market
✉	Main post office	⚓ Beach	Park
⚱	Statue/monument	Ω Cave	Pedestrian area
🏛	Museum/gallery	▲ Summit	Urban area
📖	Library	✳ Viewpoint	Non-urban area
🎭	Theatre	🏰 Castle	National park
		✚ Cathedral/church	Transport hub